The Economics of Values-Based Organizations

T0270885

This book looks at the governance of values-based organizations (VBOs), which are organizations with a mission and identity based on ideals. Examples of VBOs include non-profit organizations, charities, NGOs, environmental, educational or cultural organizations, and social enterprises. The main objective of any VBO is to evolve and grow without losing its identity, which its survival is linked to in the medium and long terms.

The focus of this book is the study of the relational and motivational dynamics during identity crisis, using critical mass models and Hirschman's "exit and voice" framework.

This book analyses the dynamics that arise in VBOs when the quality of the ideal deteriorates. On the basis of Hirschman's "exit and voice" model, it analyses the factors that lead the best members – the intrinsically motivated ones who care most about the mission and ideals of the organization – to leave if their voice is ignored. We show that the possible cumulative effects caused by the "exit" of intrinsically motivated members can lead the organization to a process of deterioration.

This book offers an analysis of these phenomena, which are usually studied in sociology or political science, by using an economic approach and the language of evolutionary game theory. By combining sociological politics and economics as a theoretical tool, we create a fresh approach to explore crises in organizations.

Luigino Bruni is a Full Professor at LUMSA University, Rome, Italy.

Alessandra Smerilli is an Associate Professor at PFSE-Auxilium University, Rome, Italy.

Routledge Advances in Social Economics
Edited by John B. Davis
Marquette University

This series presents new advances and developments in social economics thinking on a variety of subjects that concern the link between social values and economics. Need, justice and equity, gender, cooperation, work poverty, the environment, class, institutions, public policy and methodology are some of the most important themes. Among the orientations of the authors are social economist, institutionalist, humanist, solidarist, cooperatist, radical and Marxist, feminist, post-Keynesian, behaviouralist, and environmentalist. The series offers new contributions from today's foremost thinkers on the social character of the economy.

Published in conjunction with the Association of Social Economics.

Previous books published in the series include:

1. Social Economics
Premises, findings and policies
Edited by Edward J. O'Boyle

2. The Environmental Consequences of Growth
Steady-state economics as an alternative to ecological decline
Douglas Booth

3. The Human Firm
A socio-economic analysis of its behaviour and potential in a new economic age
John Tomer

4. Economics for the Common Good
Two centuries of economic thought in the humanist tradition
Mark A. Lutz

5. Working Time
International trends, theory and policy perspectives
Edited by Lonnie Golden and Deborah M. Figart

6. The Social Economics of Health Care
Edited by John Davis

7. Reclaiming Evolution
A Marxist institutionalist dialogue on social change
William M. Dugger and Howard J. Sherman

8. The Theory of the Individual in Economics
Identity and value
John Davis

The Economics of Values-Based Organizations

An introduction

Luigino Bruni and Alessandra Smerilli

Routledge
Taylor & Francis Group

LONDON AND NEW YORK

First published 2015
by Routledge
2 Park Square, Milton Park, Abingdon, Oxon OX14 4RN

and by Routledge
52 Vanderbilt Avenue, New York, NY 10017

First issued in paperback 2020

Routledge is an imprint of the Taylor & Francis Group, an informa business

British Library Cataloguing in Publication Data
A catalogue record for this book is available from the British Library

Library of Congress Cataloging in Publication Data
Bruni, Luigino, 1966-
The economics of values-based organisations : an introduction / Luigino Bruni, Alessandra Smerilli.
pages cm -- (Routledge advances in social economics)
1. Business ethics. I. Smerilli, Alessandra. II. Title.
HF5387.B784 2014
658--dc23
2014001963

ISBN 13: 978-0-367-66947-8 (pbk)

ISBN 13: 978-0-415-72335-0 (hbk)

ISBN 13: 978-1-315-78080-1 (ebk)

Typeset in Times New Roman
by GreenGate Publishing Services, Tonbridge, Kent

Contents

viii *Contents*

Figures

Introduction

A summary of this book's aims

The economy and society as a whole are going through some epochal changes, much greater and more general than just the globalization of markets. Firms and markets are growing more and more distant from the model that we once implemented in order to imagine, describe and live them just a few decades ago. In particular, we are contributing to the declining role played by technological and financial capital in the success and longevity of a business in relation to human, social and civil capital and associated goods. In a market in which the role of hierarchy, trade unions and politics—the glue that keeps firms and traditional organizations together—is changing rapidly and drastically, both small and big enterprises grow and close down (more and more largely) due to their ability or inability to keep together people with different motivations and preferences. In such a context, the scarcest resource, and thus the most fragile one, is the art of caring, of "weaving relationships," that is the ability to act in such a way that human diversity, inside and outside the organization, does not implode into chaos and anarchy but gives rise to new synergies. Even if it might seem paradoxical to the observer that follows economic and civil life through television talk shows, today more than ever market competition is influenced by the quality of the people and by the relationships among them especially when such relationships are not subject to command and obedience but are meant to be reciprocal on an egalitarian level (human beings, in fact, do not find it particularly difficult to command or obey but they do find it hard to interact with one another on a truly egalitarian level).

Even if the ancient community based on status and hierarchy has been rapidly and relentlessly declining, we have still not found new and positive forms for our life in common as equals in the family, in schools, in workplaces, in civil society and in politics. Faced with such kinds of "emptiness" today, there is a tendency to answer with mutual indifference and intolerance.

These are some of the reasons why this book talks mostly about relationships, people, motivations inside organizations and the economy, and it does so by looking at a particular type of organization that highlights the crucial role played by the person and his/her motivations. We will call this kind of organization a Values-Based Organization (VBO) that is radically a *people* and *motivation based* one and will take it as a starting point to propose some kind of initial grammar, syntax and, maybe, semantics to explain this intertwining of motivations, incentives, gratuity and cooperative behaviors: elements that are present, in different modes and measures in every organization.

As a matter of fact, organizations that are purely speculative are few and, above all, as the financial and economic crisis from which we are struggling to escape has showed us, they do not last long. The Swiss economist Bruno Frey (2009) has recently highlighted that the average life of the U.S. speculative insurances and of the investment funds that were overcome by the financial crisis is just a few years; the medieval Benedictine Abbeys in Central Europe, lasted instead, on average, for five centuries. If the Italian economy today, for example, manages to survive the big crisis through which it is going, this would be due not to the financial and speculative big capitalistic companies and banks, but to the "fabric" of small enterprises that are deep-rooted in the territory. Such enterprises have inherited the tacit culture and the knowledge produced around the abbeys and the monasteries that struggled, generated and innovated every day in order to live and that we do not consider—in their substance—to be very distant from the organizations we call VBOs. The Italian economist Giacomo Becattini writes:

> The canonic method of increasing productivity and innovation based on the raising doses of science and capital (accumulation and technological progress), suppose that the human agent participant in the productive process has a high natural capacity of adaptation to the changes provoked by science and capital-adaptation that could easily be stimulated through material incentives. This can work quite well until it is the productivity problem that predominates, and the one related to innovation is being solved in the very roots of the productive process through the use of scientific and technological procedures controlled by the capital (such as laboratories of scientific research, market research etc.); once that the innovation problem which implies more complex behaviors gains relevance, though, both the control mechanisms and the material incentives become insufficient. What is necessary now is the "genuine participation," let's say it like this, in the enterprise's destiny, the sharing, at least broadly speaking, of the firm's strategy and the basic loyalty among the members of the productive team—qualities that

cannot always be promoted through material incentives but are rooted, instead, in the human being according to his/her lifestyle and to the environment in which he/she has grown. Such qualities are based on an organic set of values, knowledge, reactions to the external circumstances that has been slowly absorbed during the regular repeating of the ordinary situations of life. Values, knowledge and behaviors that, when shared, make it possible for the innovative entrepreneur to transmit a certain message to his/her often diffident collaborators.

(Becattini 2009, pp. 44–5)

And he adds one interesting consideration in light of the topic that we will examine in the second part of this work:

So the industrial district represents a social organism that, on the basis of certain values and historically inherited productive knowledge, sets up a sum of behaviors from the type described above. I'm not saying that each district is populated only by perfect *homines distrectuales*; I just want to say that if a consistent and qualified part of the agents of a certain district doesn't have such characteristics, the district "gets into trouble" and goes out of the population of the districts.

(ibid., p. 45)

Before starting our discourse, we have to address a basic, preliminary although necessarily rhetorical question: is there a need for a book dedicated to the VBOs, and to the relationship between ideals, organizations and economics? The main reason for our (obviously) positive answer is the conviction that the economics is not a morally neutral field in which only authorized personnel can participate. We believe that economics represents a piece of life in which men and women put into action all their passions, vices and virtues. As the many charisms of the Church, or the cooperative movement and the trade unions and the social economy, have showed us during the centuries and continue to show us today, there has always been, and there still is, a place in the economic field for the highest ideals. Those who want to tell economic history correctly, know that, in the past as in the present, in the economic field right next to the biggest sins stand also big virtues, that there are people who have rendered and continue to render it a place of authentic human and spiritual excellence—a fact proved by the life of many workers, bankers, trade union members and entrepreneurs who have been able to reach the peak of human perfection transforming their workplaces and their enterprises into real sanctuaries of the human mature.

But when the ideals penetrate the economic and civil field the human relationships get both more complex and rich: the conflicts, the risks and the mistakes increase but the same also happens with the quality of life, inside and outside the organizations. The "wounds" arise but, along with them, also come the "blessings," and it is often impossible to separate them (Bruni 2007). This work is an inquiry into the bigger complexity, but also the bigger human quality that we find in organizations (economic, social, political, religious, educational, etc.) when ideals give birth to them and nourish them, day by day, in the fascinating and surprising effort of everyday life.

The primary inspiration for the basis of this work is not the reading of books and scientific papers but real-life experience. There are two elements that link the authors: both of us work inside VBOs; both of us are scholars of economic theory. That is why it seemed a good idea to use our knowledge to bring light to an area of economic and social theory that has not been explored enough—one that concerns the typical dynamics experienced in organizations built around the adherence of their members to a common ideal. This is a natural expression of our profession, which we do not consider an "uncommitted technicism" (we use here the effective expression of Giacomo Becattini) but a civil and ethical engagement.

Such organizations can be economic ones, and thus enterprises, that differ from the enterprises seen as a number of contracts, incentives or machines that produce money (if they manage to), since they are inspired and held together by ideals and non-material motivations that interact with wages, profits, incentives and markets as well. That is why our study on VBOs is not limited to enterprises or "economic VBOs": we would like to apply it to each VBO, including ones that do not have a typically economic nature or goals such as, for example, a political party, a religious order, a cultural or environmental association, a trade union or a NGO dedicated to the promotion of human rights, whose motivational and relational dynamics can, or could, fit the models and analysis that we are about to present. We believe that such an enlargement of the field of study is needed today because one of the characteristics of post-modernity is the erasing of the border between economic and non-economic: the economic analysis, then, at least the good and non-ideological one, can turn out to be useful, always in synergy with other disciplinary fields. This is what we will try to do in the following pages by putting together the economic categories and some instruments from other fields such as psychology, history, organizational sociology and philosophy.

Among the many possible perspectives or formal objectives of a work dedicated to the issue of values-based organizations, we have decided to pay special attention to the moments of transition or those of crisis, especially the complex and problematic ones that concern identity, which is crucial for the development of every type of organization and not only VBOs. When it works out and flourishes, both the individual and the collective life can be seen as a sequence of crises that have been faced and overcome. And each crisis, an individual or a collective one, is ambivalent. It could be the beginning of a new spring, it could create the right conditions so we can find our profound vocation, but it could also make us worse and block the way to our psychological and spiritual growth. This is one more reason why we should give importance to examining the nature of relationships that occur inside such organizations in order to understand better their morphology and intervene with more effective instruments in the moments when the crisis occurs—this is crucial: almost always the starting point of a vital process is the most important one—and manage to overcome them successfully.

What is an organization?

This work is dedicated to VBOs: and, therefore, the first question which we have to ask is: what is an organization?

The answers, even the many theoretical ones, are not easy mainly because we are surrounded by organizations, today and in the past: this common and everyday experience makes it difficult to reflect on what realities such as a family, a school, a church, the army, the mafia or a Parliament all have in common. A firm or a non-profit[1] hospital, for example, represent two complex institutions founded and coordinated in order to achieve one (or more than one) goal through the use of specific structures, people and instruments. Usually, a family or a sport association is not immediately perceived as an organization because of the difficulty in defining either the specific goal which they pursue or the instruments necessary for their functioning and maintenance. But the theory of organizations could show us that such goals do exist, as well as the instruments needed to achieve them, even if they are formal and deliberated to a different extent. The hierarchy, an instrument of ancient and sacred origin, still plays a fundamental role with its symbolic function (such as the distinction between pure and impure, the immunity and interdependence that mediates them) far more important than the simple coordination or efficiency of the organizations. A fact that is often forgotten even by organizational theorists, it is worth noting that social life is not composed exclusively of organizations but a consistent part of it is also ordered according to conventions, which represent some complex actions not intentionally "created" by someone striving for a certain goal.[2]

Cooperation plays the leading role in organizations while it is less evident in conventions and normally is not the fruit of a specific intention: going out in the morning and driving our car does not require an intention to cooperate with the rest of the drivers that we meet on our way; our goal is, instead, to get to our workplace safely as soon as possible: the coopera-tion (when and where it exists) can be seen as an objective fact and not as an intentional one. We could even say that one of the important differences between organizations (the enterprises) and this eminent convention–institution (not organizations) that is the market, has something to do with cooperation–competition. It is usually considered that the market functions well when the individuals within it compete, whereas the firm is essentially cooperation. Or, to be more precise, in its internal relationships the enter-prise, seen as an organization, is mostly cooperation; while in its external relationships, thus seen as an actor in the market, it is mainly competition. In reality, such a view, which is consolidated in theory as in practice, repre-sents some weaknesses both concerning the enterprise–organization and the market–convention.

First of all, the competition plays a co-essential role inside the organi-zations as well—sometimes they can "get ill" because of an excess of competition among their members, but on other occasions this can occur because of lack of competition, which originates interpersonal dynamics that bring with them mediocrity and inefficiency. If competition is intended in the right way as *cum-petere*, as an action of "searching together" that is dif-ferent from the one related to cooperation, the comparison with others and emulating them can have a significant role in allowing me to know better my own limits and potential, just as happens in a sporting competition dur-ing which it is my rival who helps me to discover and go beyond my limits and to achieve excellence. It is competition with others that can reveal my weaknesses, my buried resources that could remain latent (especially in the young) in a context in which the only "measure" available is cooperation. Together with Giandomenico Romagnosi, Carlo Cattaneo and the entire tradition of the Civil Economy, we can call this kind of competition *civil concorrenza* (civil competition) that highlights the single individual where cooperation enhances mainly the group; a virtuous civil life, however, should improve both individual and group (and not just one of these two poles). Those who operate inside enterprises, schools, universities and various institutions are in general aware that good competition coexists with good cooperation, to which it is a complementary element and not the opposition. In some moments and stages, it is the cooperation oriented to a common goal that prevails, and in others (for example in the case of an award or a career promotion) you find yourself competing (*cum-petere*) with the same individuals with whom you cooperate in many other fields; when organiza-tions fail to move at the same time according to these two scales, seeing colleagues as both competitors *and* allies, their life becomes progressively confined to only one dimension and gets into crisis. The quality of human relations within them deteriorates and leads them along some unsustainable paths (due to certain pathologies both related to the competition and to the cooperation). The nature of the unsustainability within our organizations is not only economic, financial, environmental or energetic; there is also a certain relational and spiritual unsustainability on which a significant part of the quality of our model of development and of the joy of living our everyday private and public life is dependent.

At the same time, the market cannot be interpreted only as a matter of competition because, as classic authors such as Mill and Einaudi teach us, it is also and mainly a matter of joint cooperative actions which aim to create a mutual advantage for the parties involved and, when it works out, for the society as well. To say it in a different way, if we want to get a better understanding both of the organizations and of the market we should overcome the cooperation–competition opposition that is just one among many other dichotomies which characterize Western thought such as the soul–body, spiritual–physical, faith–reason, *eros–agape* ones. Of course, *eros* is not equivalent to *agape*, as competition is not identical to cooperation, but they are both coessential to the flourishing of human beings and communities; and it is even possible that if we decided to look more closely and observe them in the concrete historical dynamics, we would probably notice that the analogies between *eros* and gift, between competition and cooperation, are more relevant on the differences, given they all represent human "affairs" marked by the good and the bad.

These points should explain our surprise at the inattention given in the field of economic theory to the examination of organizations and their specific dynamics. Even if there was not a lack of analysis of organizations (here we can think about agency theory and the theory regarding contracts that we find in all text books of economics), today there would still be too much difference between such analysis and the quantity and quality of theory and engagement in macroeconomic and econometric research, for example. And even though we have to recognize that recently there has been an increasing interest in some organizational topics, the usual analytical approach to organizational dynamics is still not essentially different if compared to the one utilized towards other kinds of action: in other words, there is a strong tendency to read all kinds of actions in the same way, within or outside the organization, as behaviors guided by the same unique instrumental and maximizing logic. This means that the decision of an employee or a manager, for example, can be described just like a person choosing her partner, or the choice of a family regarding how many children they have, or the choice of Abraham (in the book of Genesis) to sacrifice his son Isaac. On the basis of the same idea of rationality that should be applied to every sphere of life, the way of acting inside organizations is also seen as a rational and instrumental one. Thus, there should not be any *differentia specifica* of the organized activity. But are we sure that we behave in the same way, according to the same rationality, when we change a job or when we buy a ticket on the internet? When we protest to our head-office and when we protest in a coffee shop about the poor quality of the coffee?

The economic science still pays little attention to organizations that are different from the capitalistic enterprise, and even when this is not the case, the family, the church, the State and a multinational company are all treated in the same manner. In fact, in the organizational theory today as well as in the practice, there is one quite dangerous and pernicious element that we can call organizational "reductionism" or "isomorphism."

What does this mean? There is, mainly in the Anglo-Saxon area, a quite strong tendency to deal with all kind of organizations as if they were similar or even the same.

A school and a hospital, a multinational and a cooperative enterprise, a university and a football team are all seen as expressions of the type "organization" and, thus, the methods used in order to get a better comprehension or heal them are also the same.

In our experience we have met some consultants who, on the basis of such a theory, have offered the same identical kind of courses of organizational theory, to managers of for-profit enterprises as well as to nuns in charge of the government of a religious community. Obviously there are many things in common between a commercial enterprise, a cooperative one and a religious community, but we are convinced that a good theory of organizations should concentrate mostly on the little differences that exist between the different kinds of organizations. Even though human beings and chimpanzees share 98 percent of their DNA, the 2 percent remaining is what matters when we want to understand a language, the economics or the life in common, the happiness and the unhappiness.

Hierarchy, *philia*, market, and cooperation

The hierarchy could be defined as an instrument useful to the exercise of authority, or a reciprocal relationship of supremacy and subordination on the basis of which civil, military and religious organizations can be built. The French anthropologist Louis Dumont, pupil of Marcel Mauss, has dedicated a significant part of his scientific career to the study of hierarchic societies (in particular the traditional Indian ones) and to their comparison with modern egalitarian societies. According to his definition, the hierarchy is "a scale of command in which the lowest ranks are linked to the superior ones in a regular succession" (Dumont 1980, p. 65). Originally, the meaning of the word and the concept has a religious nature. The Hindu castes in India as well as the Catholic church can be seen as exemplary domains to which we can refer to in order to understand what the hierarchy is in its essence. According to Dumont, the hierarchic societies (or caste ones that for Dumont are the archetypes of each hierarchic society) are holistic ones (it is the group that exists and not its single members), whereas the egalitarian ones are individualistic (the groups are valuable only when chosen and created freely by the individuals). The individual "is born" only when he goes out of the grid of the caste system and becomes samnyasin (ascetic). The individual that goes out of the caste's communitas does not find the community of individuals but the loneliness, the non-community.

According to Dumont, the hierarchic societies represent three characteristics that can be theoretically distinguished but that in normal societies coexist: a) the society is organized in ranks, castes and groups or classes; b) there are detailed norms which aim at the clear distinction between the classes; c) there is a strong division of labor and a strong interdependence that derives from it.

Over a hundred and fifty years ago, John S. Mill (1848) pointed out two feudal institutions that survived in modern democracy: families and capitalistic corporations. Both operated just like old feudal systems: husbands subjugated their wives in families, and corporations maintained hierarchy to regulate human relations. Mill believed women's suffrage and employment could modernize feudal families, and cooperatives could democratize businesses. Today gender equality is increasing (though not in companies); women work in politics and in the economy. However, capitalistic companies are still hierarchical. Although corporations are essential institutions in modern democracy, they have not overcome the outdated principles of hierarchy. We have accepted this modern paradox in silence and without the much needed public debate. On the other hand, the cooperative movement has promoted democratic corporations (in addition to fair consumption and savings).

The return of corporate hierarchy on its own is worrisome; it is the combination of hierarchy tied to sound principles, like *philia*, that enable healthy development. *Philia*, an Aristotelian word, means friendship and informal reciprocity. To be successful, organizations should bring workers together in the pursuit of common goals for the common good. Vertical corporations do not work well because they exclude most of the workers from decision-making. Though they may make profit and employ people, these corporations inhibit employees' personal development and well-being. As in every social relationship, corporations have an impact on their workers' emotions, passions, hopes and love; businesses must move beyond narrow self interest actions. *Philia* among workers and directors assures enthusiasm and graciousness, which are qualities that foster innovations and help overcome economic crises.

Originally hierarchy existed to protect the pure people from the impure. Both archaic organizations and capitalistic corporations built vertical structures to assure privilege. Like the institutions of old, today's top managers avoid any contact with the proletariat. Hierarchy (the tool for the creation of *immunitas*) without reciprocity (*communitas*) creates vertical and hostile companies.

In companies where entrepreneurs and employees were old friends who worked side by side (often as craftsmen), participative management produced good products and created a strong sense of well-being. As far as decision-making, reprimands, responsibilities, duties, salary and risks are concerned, managers are different from employees. However, all workers share and fight for the same ultimate goal: the prosperity of businesses, communities, families and the fulfillment of their dreams.

Entrepreneurs, directors and employees have different roles set by corporate hierarchy and contracts; however, *philia* and implicit mutual agreements (as important as contracts) can bring them together as equals. This corporate solidarity can bring a humane and pleasant life to all. Equality within companies allows people to reach their full potential. Relations among equals produce true happiness; the eye to eye contact between men (Adam) and women (Eve) fills them with joy and wonder. If formal and vertical relations replace *philia* within organizations, the joyful and entertaining atmosphere disappears.

Company parties are very useful and, unfortunately, very rare. Bosses play around, drink and eat with workers, bringing everyone together. If they do not engage with their workers, then even Christmas celebrations can reinforce distinctions, hierarchy and privilege. Although hierarchy is essential when managing a sinking ship, it is not the most effective way out of crises. During times of calm, companies and communities must invest in *philia* and reciprocity. A vertical structure can save companies and communities from hardship, but they need the workers' hearts and souls to overcome great crises. Contracts and organization charts cannot assure this as well as informal pacts. *Philia* is stronger than blunt commands—although it is more familiar and "contaminated"; it bears moral power, which is collectively recognized. This power, built on everyday experience, comes from the awareness of people's common fragility and vulnerability.

Farmers and women of the past (and present) are familiar with this invisible power. *Philia* transforms hierarchy into a more humane, brotherly and stronger structure. Like in Adriano Olivetti's businesses, this strength springs from the corporate operations, governance, rules and fair wages that are inspired by *philia*. Friendly and generous entrepreneurs are stronger than unsociable privileged bosses. Despite that, business schools do not teach these qualities. Capitalistic professors condemn and discourage friendship and solidarity; they consider these to be abilities for "losers." However, these attributes are like birch trees, which seem very frail but are stronger than the robust pines when resisting stormy winds. The world's stormy economy and tormented civil society exhort us to investment in personal relations and in a new organizational culture. We need to appeal to the power of birch trees.

In praise of biodiversity

The globalization today brings about a strong tendency to the leveling and standardization of organizational tools but, if we do not give importance to the 2 percent that demonstrates the difference, we will not be able anymore to identify the crucial elements that characterize each organization such as its culture, its values, its mission. It is possible that the organization of a cooperative differs by only 2 percent or 10 percent from the one of a capitalistic enterprise, but when consultants and managers deal with it in the same manner, using the same instruments, they are erasing centuries of history, of freedom, of civilization and, in this way, are guiding it towards unsustainable paths.

Life is nourished and grows thanks to diversity: this is one of the great messages of biology. A civil society grows well when it makes possible the existence of more different types of organizations, when it respects and fosters their specificity and culture.

Democracy and economic and social freedom are guaranteed by the plurality of organizational forms: the whole economy and society become poorer when they lose their VBOs if they turn, for example, into speculative ones or they quit their activity because of bad management or consulting. Life is richer, the social ecosystem is full of biodiversity, cultural variety and life when there are multiple organizations present in it, rooted in different realities, and among them many VBOs.

In fact, every VBO is different from all the others because, according to our cultural perspective, each of them is born of a specific *charisma* (a gift), embodied in one or more persons—a fact that gives it a unique tone in the concert of the life in common. With the concept of charisma we intend to represent the gift of "different eyes" that make it possible for some to see resources and beautiful things where others see only problems. This charismatic dimension[3] of VBOs will be present in all our work. It is, at the same time, their main strength and their main weakness; from one point of view, it fills up the organization with ideals and passion and thus with life and happiness; from another point of view, it renders more difficult the transmission of such a dimension from one generation to another, complicating the handling of relational conflicts and the replacement of some key figures on which depends the survival in time of the whole organization.

This book wants to contribute to the better comprehension of this vital tension inside such kinds of organizations, of the crises that characterize them; it aims to improve the quality of people and relationships within VBOs, and, thus, within the economy and civil society as well.

Finally, even though we talk about organizations, the big challenges faced by the life in common remain the background of this essay. In particular, we would like to allocate our analysis within a reflection on fraternity. One last note on this. If we look at the history of the different communities or movements that have tried to foster a fraternal, egalitarian and non-hierarchic kind of social relation, we come upon one constant element: whenever these communities and movements had given birth to institutions, the passage from the "charisma" to its "institutionalization" (as Max Weber defines it) has always been a delicate, crucial and decisive moment in their development.

In their "institutionalization," the principles and practices of fraternity and equality systematically come up against the need for coordination, order and supervision common in the organizational dynamics. Such tension will be present during our whole journey and will remain an open question until the end.

Fraternity is the forgotten principle of the modern age. In fact, while freedom and equality have become its big projects, fraternity is the one which has remained incomplete, assigned, probably, only to the private and communitarian sphere without turning into a civil and political category. Why? The reason can be found in the fact that, unlike the other two principles, it is not an individual condition or state, but a bond, a relational good. I cannot enjoy it by myself and defend it from others since it flourishes when we are able to grow together, overcoming the wounds that each fraternity brings within itself. While equality and freedom are perfectly compatible with the individualistic humanism, fraternity requires a relational vision of the life in common—a vision that is becoming distant from our wealthy societies but, at the same time, yearned for by a society composed of human beings increasingly full of goods but more and more lonely.

Map

The book begins with a short presentation of the so-called tradition of Civil Economy, a Neapolitan and Italian stream of modern social and economic thinking, that is important in order to properly contextualize our discourse on motivation, gratuity and reciprocity. In Chapter 2, by a discussion of the contemporary debate on the economics of caring, we present our vision of the market as a mutual advantage—neither egoism, nor altruism. The VBOs enter the stage in Chapter 3, when we introduce the issue, giving a special emphasis to gratuity (an original Italian word, very difficult to translate into English), and its special connection with an even more odd word, *agape.* Chapter 4 is devoted to the personnel selection process in VBOs, due to the importance to select members (at least some of them) with some dimension of "vocation." Chapters 5 and 6 contain the analytical part of the book, that is a creative combination of O.A. Hirschman's theory of *Exit, Voice and Loyalty* (Chapter 5) applied to VBOs, and the models of critical mass (Chapter 6). The success of the operation attempted in this book depends chiefly on these two central chapters, and in our rhetorical capacity to convince colleagues and readers that a combination Hirschman-Schelling can have something relevant and new to say to the theory of organizations (in general, not only to VBOs). In Chapter 7 we go deeper into a crucial issue in organizations, in particular during or before relational crises: the importance of distinguishing "good" (constructive) voice from the "bad" (opportunistic) ones. Finally, in Chapter 8 we present the main theses of the book by using a different (but powerful) language, that of (basic) network analysis. The conclusion is more than standard ending remarks; it is an attempt at synthesis, with a language more affected by philosophy and even biblical studies, a discourse which focuses on the dimension of the vulnerability and fragility of goodness, presented as the human condition, within and outside VBOs. Finally, in the Appendix, we present a more analytical version of the "three types" members model that are at the center of our theory of VBOs.

The primary focus of this book is on *crises* within organizations, motivational and relational crises in particular. How to anticipate and prevent such crises, and how to avoid degenerating processes, can be considered our main challenge, and maybe its most relevant contribution.

Notes

1 Although if sometimes we use, for making easy the argument, the expression "non-profit," it is important to specify that the distinction of organizations into "for" and "not" profit is not a good one or adequate to understand what happens in many social realities, especially in VBOs.
2 The traffic jam, for example, is a typical case in which we encounter these conventions: nobody has created it according to a specific purpose (in fact, in our big cities it would be an invention of a quite perverse mind) but it is, instead, the fact that emerges from the evolution of millions of individual actions that have different goals (those who go out to work in the morning and those who go out to visit a friend, etc.). As with organizations the conventions also need some instruments for their maintenance and efficiency, but their nature is quite different (in the urban traffic jam, for example, there is no hierarchy even if there is an authority that is external to the drivers). Another example of a convention is the language (who has created it? what was their goal?), currency, etc.
3 Concerning this meaning of "charisma," which is quite different from the usual "biblical" one, we refer to Bruni-Smerilli (2008) and Bruni-Sena (2012).

1   Market and human relations

> Our age is carrying out a process of real liquidation not only in the business world but in the one of ideas as well. The price of each thing is so vile that I wonder if there will be someone ready to pay.
>
> (S. Kierkegaard)

Market and civilization

We start our journey adopting a perspective of economy and of the market inspired by the tradition known as Civil Economy. Such a broad subject could seem to be a useless digression in a study, as the present one, whose main arguments concern VBOs. We believe, instead, that before we start a book on ideals and economic life, it is necessary to face some basic questions that will serve as a background to our whole study: is the existence of VBOs, that is of actors open to dimensions different from sole self-interest, just a remnant of the past? Or could the "normal," "ordinary" market and economy host behaviors moved by motivations different from the ones considered to be normal in economics (such as self-interests, instrumentality, etc.)? In other words: in what conditions can a VBO be seen as an integral part of a post-modern and globalized economy? Is it just an anomaly, an exception?

In order to answer this question, we find it useful to make a brief incursion into the history of economic thought.

Political Economy as a systematic and autonomous reflection based on the assumption that only self-interests and administration of justice were necessary for the achievement of the "common good" (the Wealth of the Nations) was founded in eighteenth century Europe. The leading theorist of this vision was the Scottish philosopher and economist Adam Smith. In the same period as Smith's work, in Naples Antonio Genovesi[1] and some other philosophers, jurists and reformers were theorizing the market (which, as a matter of fact, did not exist in that time) in a different way, according to a humanist and Christian philosophical approach based on concepts such as reciprocity and "mutual assistance." According to Genovesi, as well as the modern tradition of Civil Economy founded by him, the market represents a field whose fundamental law is reciprocity, just as it is in the rest of the life in common, and in which it is possible to pursue the common good, thus, the good of all.

By concentrating on mutual assistance and advantage, the Civil Economy invited us to look at the market (and at civil society in general) as a broad space in which it was possible to grasp the opportunities of exchange in order to obtain an overall benefit (among which the main and most important benefit consisted in the creation of markets and institutions that would replace the feudal ones).[2]

If we were to consider the market in this way, it would be easier to understand what kind of connection exists between self-interest and common good, since in this case the intention of the individual is oriented simultaneously to his/her personal advantage and to one of the others involved in the market exchange. Indeed, according to the classical vision of Smith and of Political Economy, the only virtues "required" by the individual are prudence, industriousness and illuminated sense of his/her self-interest—virtues typical of the prudent man (to use Smith's expression) which make him understand, on the basis of his own experience and those of others, that shortsighted opportunism is not profitable in the long run. As the "invisible hand" metaphor tells us with extreme clarity, common good is the indirect and not intentional result of the actions of numerous individuals seeking their own profit: it represents a kind of laic providence that guides private intentions, aimed to self-interest, towards the common good and this happens regardless of the awareness of the individuals who, in this way, unconsciously become collaborators to the overall wealth (Bruni 2012a).

People act in order to satisfy their own interests in the best possible way but, as a result of some kind of deception of the reason, these private interests produce effects that were neither predicted, nor desired by the agents who providentially generate common good as it is evident in this passage of "The Wealth of Nations":

A revolution of the greatest importance to the public happiness was in this manner brought about by two different orders of people who had not the least intention to serve the public. To gratify the most childish vanity was the sole motive of the great proprietors. The merchants and artificers, much less ridiculous, acted merely from a view to their own interest, and in pursuit of their own pedlar principle of turning a penny wherever a penny was to be got. Neither of them had either knowledge or foresight of that great revolution which the folly of the one, and the industry of the other, was gradually bringing about.

(1976, pp. 389–90)

In the past as in the present, in Civil Economy's tradition there is a different type of relationship between private intentions and common good: there is a direct link between the intentions of the single agents and the effects of their actions. There is no need to "reverse intentions" or to create a tension between the two levels (private and public) of good (something that reminds us of Mandeville's "private vices and public virtues"), since individuals intend and seek the common good *intentionally*.

Here we find the roots of reciprocity and fraternity seen as a market paradigm, one typical assumption in Illuminist Naples: the market has a moral content (and morality implies directly the specific role of intentions) and such moral sense has to be encouraged, interiorized and made explicit in those societies which function well.

Civil Economy

The tradition of the so-called Civil Economy that flourishes in the eighteenth century in Italy (Naples, Milan, Tuscany and Venice) should be interpreted as the modern expression of the civil tradition started during the Middle Ages in the Benedictine Abbeys, in the *studia* of the Franciscans and of the Dominicans and in the great age of the Tuscan civil humanism, afterwards. According to Genovesi, as well as the first humanists, civil life is not simply not contradicting good life, but is even seen as the space in which both private and public happiness can be fully obtained as a result of the good and fair laws, commerce and the civil institutions in which human beings exercise their sociality: "even if the companionship can sometimes produce/cause some bad results, at the same time it is also the one who insures the life and the goods: something which pleasures are unknown to the humans in nature" (Genovesi 1973[1766], p. 37).

In Genovesi's vision economic relationships in the market are those characterized by "mutual assistance." They are not, thus, impersonal and anonymous. Indeed, market is itself seen as an expression of the general law of civil society which is reciprocity. This fact appears with particular evidence in his analysis of the trust or of "public trust," that we would call today "social capital" (Bruni and Sugden 2000) that is at the center of his lectures of Civil Economy and of the whole reformatting program of Naples.

According to the view of Civil Economy, development, markets and the entire economic life represent a question of *fides*, of trust. One of its basic concepts is, indeed, the "public trust" which is seen by Genovesi and the Civil Economy tradition as the real pre-condition of economic development: "confidence is the soul of commerce … without it all the parts that build up its structure would collapse by themselves" (Filangieri 2003[1780], p. 93).

If it is true that the development of markets brings with itself civil and economic development, in the Neapolitan vision it is even more urgent to underline that the cultivation of public trust is the pre-condition to every economic and civil progress: "nothing is more useful to one big and fast circulation than the public trust" (*Lezioni*, II, cap.10, 1). It is important, then, what Genovesi specifies in the footnote: "The word fides means a rope that links and unifies. Thus, the public trust is the bond of families in a companionship life."

Reciprocity is a crucial category in Genovesi's and Civil Economy's vision in regard to the market. In his analysis of public trust he systematically links the concept of trust with the ones of reciprocal confidence, mutual assistance and friendship maintaining that they are all essential for the economic and civil development of society.[3]

Even if from a different perspective (at least in some sense) if compared to the one of Civil Economy, the interest in the issue of reciprocity is re-emerging today. The dimension of genuine reciprocity present in a reciprocal behavior is measured in models of the so called, strong reciprocity, through the willingness to support the sacrifice of "material" benefits in order to reward or punish the other party at one's own expense. We do not want to deny that the act of rewarding or punishing others also has a civil function (we can think here of those who, at their own risk, scold someone for throwing rubbish on the street), but at the same time we would like to stress that reciprocity represents a relationship and not a sum of preferences or of behaviors of single individuals. We should note that such theories of reciprocity are still essentially individualistic, even though individual preferences according to them could be of an altruistic or pro-social kind.

One of the consequences of such an approach is that reciprocity is interpreted as a "gift exchange": the only one to be seen as pure and genuine reciprocity, while other forms of exchange of contracts, markets and "normal" economy are defined as "bad" reciprocity, since they are self-interested and non-altruistic. A great part of Communitarian thought today goes in this direction,[4] referring to Aristotle's vision which is considered to be the father of such tradition (Bruni 2010). It is a pity that, as a matter of fact, Aristotle did not see things like that: according to him, reciprocity, the *antipeponthos*, was in the Nicomachean Ethics the "social bond," the one that holds together the polis, a reciprocity that in his vision goes from the market to the *philia*. Also the Latin word *reciprocitate* etymologically derives from rectus+procus+cum: what comes and goes, leaves and comes back mutually. Much more than a "gift exchange" which is, of course, one form of reciprocity but not the only one. Most of all, the gift should not be seen on a theoretical as well as practical level in opposition to reciprocity (where you give and you receive) and to various kinds of economic reciprocities (that exist in enterprises, contracts and markets), because in this way we would not just lose our ability to understand some important civil phenomena, but we would also confine good reciprocity to an extremely narrow field of civil and economic life; we could think here, among many different experiences, of the Fair Trade, the Economy of Communion, the Micro-finance and Microcredit in which people get help in order to get out of various poverty and exclusion traps not in the form of unconditional gifts, but with the use of contracts (even though spurred on by gratuity in the sense that we are going to give it in this book). We believe that only one multidimensional reciprocity that goes from gift exchange to contracts and rules, which is one and many at the same time, could be really sustainable and authentically human also inside the organizations, VBOs included (Bruni 2008).

Social sciences today urge one non-dichotomous way of thinking in order to get a better understanding of both of the realities, which we come across in the theory whose driving forces are more complex than the profit, and of the market and of civil life which turn out to be one not authentically human experience when they do not let reciprocity and gratuity penetrate them in the long run. Of course, a gift is not equivalent to a contract: however, both of them could be forms of good reciprocity (as they could both turn out to be forms of bad reciprocity when the contract hides exploitation of the fragile one and the gift-*munus (obligation)* disguises relationships of power and dependence).

An historical and religious element that has chiefly contributed to the rise of the dichotomy gift-market was the "trauma" caused by the act of selling and granting indulgences that played the leading (although not the only) role in the Protestant (Lutheran) Reformation. In front of a church that was pretending to sell even God's grace (*charis*, gratuity, gift)[5] and to use money for reducing or eliminating years of purgatory, and that had instituted a whole system of penances that it was possible to exchange for money, the protestant world was built on the sound distinction or separation between market and gratuity—an application of the Lutheran (Saint Augustinian) "Doctrine of the two reigns." During the economic activity, business is business, and only in a second stage, which is clearly distinguished by the first one, it is possible to donate part of the fruits of business in the form of donations, foundations, philanthropy. This is the model of "philanthropic capitalism" inspired by the Protestantism which is typical in North-American culture—the one in which was born and developed the official tradition of modern economic science. Bill Gates, for example, as an individual makes philanthropy through his foundations and Microsoft as an institution makes business. In the Middle Ages the relationship between gift and market was far more complex: it would be enough to think about the Franciscan order which formed the first systematic economic reflection on as well as the first cooperative banks (*Monti di Pietà*) (Bruni-Smerilli 2008).

Medieval humanism represented a weaving of saints and merchants, monks and labor, economy and cities. Even though their paths and theological motivations were different, the catholic reaction to the Reformation, the so-called Counter-Reformation, in regard to the relationship between economy and gift led to a result similar to the protestant one. In the seventeenth and eighteenth centuries, Europe became the scene of a process of re-feudalization, of return-to-land and blood nobility and, consequently, of reinforced defiance of the economic and civil life: to such aspects is related also to Mediterranean Europe's different economic history, its backwardness and its potential not still expressed.

Market and cooperation: U.S. and Europe compared

The division of labor in markets and in society at large is a great unintentional and implicit cooperation; the division of labor inside the company, however, is the strong sense of cooperation, a joint voluntary action. The Anglo-Saxon, protestant type of capitalism has given rise to a dichotomous model, a new edition of the Lutheran (and Augustinian) *Two Kingdoms Doctrine*. In the markets there is implicit cooperation, which is "weak" and non-intentional; in the company and in organizations in general we find explicit cooperation instead, which is strong and purposeful—two types of cooperation, two "cities" that are profoundly and naturally different from each other. This cooperation, however, is not the only possible type in the markets. The European, and particularly the Latin version of cooperation in the markets was different, because its cultural and religious matrix was not individualistic but communal. Here, the distinction between ad intra cooperation (inside company) and ad extra cooperation (in the markets) has never prevailed—at least until recently. Family businesses (90 percent of the private sector in Italy is still composed by these), cooperatives, Adriano Olivetti can all be explained by taking seriously the cooperative and communal nature of the economy. This is why the European cooperative movement has been the most typical expression of market economy in Europe. Just as the industrial districts (from the township of Prato and yarn to Fermo and shoes) are (and were) such, where entire communities have become an economy without ceasing to be a community. Thus, the model of the U.S. capitalism is the anonymous market and it seeks to "marketize" (render into market) even the company, which is increasingly seen as a nexus of contracts, a "commodity" (merchandise), or a market with "internal" vendors and customers.

The European model, however, has always tried to "communitize" (render into community) the market, taking the mutual and communal type as a model of good economy, exporting it from the company to the whole of civilized life (credit and consumer unions). Taking the costs and benefits of doing this results in a type of economy that is filled with humanity and the joy of living, but also with those wounds that fully human encounters inevitably bring about.

Today the U.S. model is colonizing the last of the territories of the European economy, also because our tradition of community and cooperation has not always lived up to the cultural and practical standards, it has not developed in all regions. The "Great Crisis" we are living now, however, tells us that the economy and society based on cooperation-without-touching-each-other may produce monsters, and that business that is only business becomes anti-business eventually. The ethos of the West is a network of strong and weak instances of cooperation of individuals that flee from the bonds of the community in search of freedom, as well as people who bind themselves of their own accord in order to live freely. In a phase of history where the pendulum of the global market tends to move towards individuals-without-ties, Europe must remember the inherently civil and social nature of economy by taking care of it and by living it.

Notes

1 Some biographical notes on Antonio Genovesi. He was born on the 1st November 1713 in the little town near Salerno Castiglione (today Castiglione del Genovesi) in an impoverished noble family. He was dedicated to the ecclesiastic life since his youth and was ordinate a priest in 1737. After he had lived a few years in Buccino (SA), in 1738 he moved to Naples. There he studied philosophy attending Vico's classes whose thought would have remained a source of inspiration for him also in the future. In 1739, he founded a private school where philosophy and theology were taught and where he started to mature his experience as an educator. In this period, he met Celestino Galiani who helped him to obtain in 1745 his first job as a professor in metaphysics. Meanwhile, in 1743, he had published the first part of Elementa metaphysicae—a philosophical work which was harshly attacked by the ecclesiastical environment. He built a relationship also with Ludovico Antonio Muratori who was another important author of the "public happiness," and got into the club of Bartolomeo Intieri who, with his Galilean approach to science, played an important role in Genovesi's transition from metaphysics to economics, from a "metaphysician to a merchant (mercatante)" (cf. Bellamy 1987). In 1753, he published the notice (manifesto) of the reformation program of the club: Discorso sopra il vero fine delle lettere e delle scienze. Between 1765 and 1769 (the year in which he died) Genovesi published his most important works: *Lezioni di economia civile* (in three editions from 1765 and 1770, quoted in the text as Lezioni).
2 Genovesi's polemic against the assistance to the poor is well known: his political ideas consisted in the creation of job opportunities for them and bringing them in this way out of the feudal logic of benefactors and assisted ones.
3 In continuity with Montesquieu, Kant, the Scottish and Milanese school, also the Neapolitan tradition considers the economic activity to be an expression of

the civil life; it sees in the commerce a civilizing factor. Just like for the civil humanists, also for Genovesi and the Neapolitans civil life is not simply not in contrast with virtue, but is even the place where virtue can be fully expressed . Furthermore, according to Genovesi and to many of the European Enlightenment philosophers from his generation, one of the fruits of commerce is the fact of bringing the nations involved in it towards peace ... war and commerce are opposite motion and rest (Lezioni, I, ch.19, VII, p. 290).

4 On the issue of communitarianism and the irreconcilable contrast between the logic of gift and the economic one see Anderson (1993).

5 We are conscious that the issue of the indulgences and the following Reformations is far more complex and cannot be explained using only the element that we are highlighting here.

2 Care and the market

Society may subsist among different men, as among different merchants, from a sense of its utility, without any mutual love or affection; and though no man in it should owe any obligation, or be bound in gratitude to any other, it may still be upheld by a mercenary exchange of good offices according to an agreed valuation. Society, however, cannot subsist among those who are at all times ready to hurt and injure one another … Beneficence, therefore, is less essential to the existence of society than justice. Society may subsist, though not in the most comfortable state, without beneficence; but the prevalence of injustice must utterly destroy it.

(Adam Smith 1759)

The health-care market and fraternity

In this chapter, adopting a (European) concept not defined by the dichotomous view of reciprocity and gratuity, we undertake one different analysis of the caring relationships which may be interpreted as a form of reciprocity or fraternity. In the second part of the chapter we will focus on an application of the Civil Economy's perspective in a field of great importance for VBOs: the socio-economic sphere of health care that is becoming more and more crucial both for civil life and economy. Questions regarding the morality, the "tone of affection" and the non-opportunistic behavior of the agents are salient when the market enters into the field of provision of personal health-care services to our parents, children, to us.

There is general concern today with the arrival of market mechanisms into new spheres (education, care) very relevant from the point of view of relationships and motivations. We are convinced that a market and economy seen from the perspective of Civil Economy can offer new elements of hope when we are trying to figure out how can we reconcile the needs of a market that continues to expand and the needs that must be met in the case of relational goods and of emotions (attention, respect, recognition).[1]

Nowadays, care services which in the past used to be provided by families (usually by female relatives), communities, churches (nuns) have become increasingly supplied by the market and by paid workers. At the same time, workers within such sectors (education, health-care) used to be seen in traditional societies as an expression of a kind of "vocation," thus it was obvious that they were not led by monetary incentives and motivations only. However, when we refer to these "relationship-sensitive" professions we still expect that this kind of "surplus" to the salary can still be found in their objective function (even though we are more disenchanted and cynical if compared to 30 years ago). We can get a full comprehension of the essence of this problem only if and when we entrust our child to a day care center or our parent to a nursing home.

In the third chapter of this book, we will present one recent attempt of economic theory to explain how it could be possible to somehow hold together these two dimensions: market and vocations—a theoretical attempt that is not entirely convincing even if deserves to be known and analyzed. In this chapter, we will try to draft a general theoretical discourse on the caring relationship adopting the Civil Economy's perspective.

This branch of economic literature supposes that the firm makes the assumption that a candidate with a vocation is not interested in salary or material incentives of a given job only (that is the point of view of standard economic theory) but assigns a certain intrinsic value to the activity which he/she applies for that is a part of the satisfaction (or utility) deriving from it. In other words, the vocation is expressed in an intrinsic reward (and not in a monetary or material one) that the individual gets by performing this specific kind of work.

As we will see more analytically and diffusely from now on, when there is a motivation present, the amount of the wage is not the only decisive factor for the candidates.

Market as an opportunity to grow together

In light of the issue of caring services, we go back to the idea of the market that emerges from Civil Economy's tradition to which our work is linked. First of all, the Civil Economy's vision invites us to look at the market as a form of reciprocity.

From the perspective of Genovesi and Dragonetti, and of authors today such as Sugden and Sen, the market represents a social mechanism which can be seen also as a reward of the civil virtues, when it functions correctly. We can read the market from a point of view that is quite unusual today but used to be common in the eighteenth century and in John Stuart Mill's work, as a remuneration system of the activities which are socially virtuous but scarce due to insufficient motivations and intrinsic rewards. If we suppose the existence of a world in which there are no markets and everyone is performing only the kind of activities that he/she loves and feels as a vocation, activities that bring intrinsic rewards, we would be faced with an excessive supply of intrinsically rewarding activities (if compared to the demand of society) and of an insufficient supply of very useful but less rewarding per se activities (such as street cleaners, laborers, mineworkers).

In general, the market offers extrinsic rewards to activities that we would not carry out, or at least not enough to satisfy the needs of society, if we were to follow only the joy derived from such an activity. Through price mechanism, the market makes it possible to reward not only those activities which we perform because *we like them* but also the ones considered to be useful by the other parties of an exchange (who therefore reward us for such activities).

From this point of view, the market represents also a mechanism that gives us signals of social scarcity, that tells us if the things which we like interest also—and mainly—somebody else; for this reason it can be seen as a form of reciprocity and social bond as well. Therefore, the market makes it possible to perform in a free and respectable way activities useful to the common good. One more reason to say that market, civil virtues, free human cooperation and common good are not necessarily opposing terms, a well-known fact in the Civil Economy tradition.[2]

We can say something more. We take as a starting point the well-known "trust game" (see Figure 2.1) as it offers us some interesting hints in order to think over the Civil Economy's specific approach.

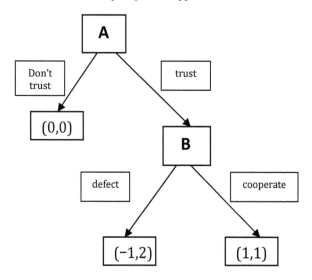

Figure 2.1 Trust game

Let us assume an individual called A (Anna) finds an offer on the internet of an antique stamp which belongs to B (Bruno)—an individual who
lives in another continent. Anna has to send the payment first and Bruno
will then send her the stamp. It is the case of a contract without a legal
enforcement (which would significantly increase the transaction costs)
so the only possibility for Anna in order to get the stamp is to trust Bruno
and pay, expecting to receive the stamp by mail. If Anna puts her trust in
Bruno and he behaves correctly, they will make an exchange and move
from the status quo (in which nothing happens: 0,0) to a situation of
mutual advantage (1,1). However, if Anna puts herself in Bruno's shoes,
she realizes that, if he decides to behave in an opportunistic way and not
to send her the stamp, once he has received the payment, he would get a
bigger advantage (2>1) and Anna would therefore find herself without
a stamp and without money (−1). Standard game theory shows us that
Anna's rational choice in this case would be not to start the deal, not
to trust him and close the game in (0,0) (0>−1). This is the situation in
the cases in which the hazardous trust is overborne by the distrust that
blocks individuals and nations in poverty traps.

How could we read this game from a civil perspective? Comparing the
two possible results: the status quo (0,0) and the pure advantage if the deal
gets closed (1,1): the market is a place of opportunities for mutual advantage, in which people can grow together and pass from a worse to a better
condition for both parties. There is only one condition required in order
that this happens: the need to "overcome the temptation to behave in an
opportunistic way in a future stage of the relation." The risky trust is a necessary condition, but the market exchange should not be interpreted as one
in which an individual has to sacrifice in order to reward the other party (B
who renounces 1 in order to reward A who has taken the risk of trust), but
as an opportunity to improve both and together.

When it is the distrust or the concern of the future gains (how we will
divide tomorrow the cake that we generate together today?) that prevail,
instead, we often end up not starting any economic and civil activity,
blocked in a situation of underdevelopment. The path of development and
life is the one that brings us from (0,0) to (1,1). The comparison (1,1) vs
(−1,2), instead, is the one that predominates in competing and position sensitive individuals and nations not able to see life in common as a sum of
opportunities to grasp, who do not perceive the world as production and
innovation, as potential "future cakes" to make but, on the contrary, as a
static reality populated by "clever" and "foolish" human beings who have
to grab pieces of the cakes made by others—a behavior that in the long run
produces only individual and collective pointlessness and blocks up everyone in the status quo (0,0).

But we can say something more with regard to market, VBOs and social entrepreneurs and we will not do so by starting from the views of a "civil" economist from the past but from one of the classical mainstream economists, David Ricardo. In 1817, the eminent English economist formulated one of the first real economic theories (since not-immediate) which is still relevant today.

Absolute advantages:

England	Portugal
Silk: 5	Silk: 8
Wine: 6	Wine: 5

Ricardo proved that even in *the case in which only relative advantages exists*, exchange is still convenient to both the parties:

Relative advantages:

England	Portugal
Silk: 5	Silk: 8
Wine: 6	Wine: 7

Ricardo has showed us that even in a world in which England is more efficient than Portugal in both of the productive sectors, it could be still more convenient for it to specialize in the sector in which it is relatively stronger and—this is the point—even in this case the exchange with the "weaker" gives advantage to the "stronger." The classic example is the one of the lawyer who, although he can type faster than a secretary, however sees an advantage in hiring one so he can focus on the legal practices (that is the concept known today as "opportunity cost"). But just as in the England/Portugal scenario, the lawyer is not performing an act of "assistance" or charity by hiring a secretary less good than him/her, but is benefitting from this exchange as well as (the secretary). When the market functions like this and includes the weaker who become an opportunity for common good, it does its job of a civilizing mechanism.

What can be the significance of such a theory for VBOs? Let us take a look at the great innovation that the emergence of social cooperation in Italy has been: the disadvantaged individuals included in an economic enterprise have often become (thanks also to a public participation in the costs, that is almost always socially efficient[3]) an occasion for a mutual advantage for the enterprise that hires them too and not a cost or act of charity.

In such cases, the person who "has been helped" feels they have participated in a reciprocal relationship which conveys greater dignity. He/she does not feel like a subject of assistance but integrated in a contract of mutual advantage, experiencing in this way more freedom and equality. Also, a person with Down syndrome can fulfill a contract of mutual advantage with a company:[4] it is necessary, though, that the entrepreneur has a real innovative capacity since the mutual advantage is always one possibility which requires a lot of work and creativity (and is not realized automatically and always), but when it comes true the market becomes a real instrument of inclusion and authentic human and civil growth. The sacrifice of the benefactor, indeed, is not always a positive signal to the recipient of the aid because it could be an expression of a power-based relationship, maybe hidden by good faith.

The civil entrepreneur should not stand still until the individuals included in his VBO feel useful for the company and for society and not just assisted by a philanthropist. Let us take into consideration the microcredit: to make those previously excluded from the credit delivery system potential recipients of banking services has been one of the main economic innovations of our times which has set free people (in particular, women) from misery and exclusion in a manner more effective than many international aids. If a certain intervention does not help all the parties involved, it could hardly be seen as genuine help to someone: the less I feel benefitted, the less I can benefit another human being and rarely can the other feel really benefitted by me, especially when the relationship lasts in time. The law of life is reciprocity that makes it possible that relations do not "get sick" but, on the contrary, grow in the presence of mutual dignity.[5] All of these considerations are consistent with the definition of the common good as the good of all and of each.

The market today is conquering an increasing area in our life penetrating the most intimate zones of interpersonal relations. We can try to defend ourselves and live such a transition as a necessary evil. Or we can try to make, instead, baby-sitters, nannies, nurses and teachers precious allies in a new social pact according to which we interpret and live also the market as a piece of life, as Civil Economy where its reciprocity can become subsidiary to the one of friendship and even of *agape*; where you can and you should pay a nurse or a baby-sitter and, at the same time, establish with them a relationship which is automatically and directly human and moral, a relationship of friendship and mutual advantage.

A preliminary conclusion

The considerations made in this chapter should not make us deny that in market relations, and especially those in the case of caring services (within or outside the market) sacrifice and intrinsic motivations are needed. We even believe exactly the opposite and everything that will be written in the next chapters, as has already been done in some other works of ours, strongly emphasizes it. The workers with vocations are important and in some cases essential, and everyone who comes into contact with such people benefits from it, both inside and outside the organizations. To have an intrinsic motivation in your job and to sacrifice yourself for others going beyond the contract, is one of the most passionate human experiences that often transform the workplace into a more human and livable space for the ones who have such a vocation and for all the others who surround them. However, the thesis that we have tried to discuss in this chapter is different: although we hope that many will be the ones who live the market relations as a chance to express their real vocation, as a sacrifice and gift of themselves, we believe that in many cases the market can also be imagined as civil and civilizing, one genuinely moral zone even when these dimensions (that can be present only in some moments in life and in some individuals) are missing or, at least, are not essential for everyone.

Why shouldn't we consider genuinely moral, for example, the behavior of a caregiver who looks after the elderly (making it possible for many of us to develop our interests and humanity) "only" for the money that they receive? Is working with accuracy even abroad in order to maintain one's own family not one completely moral activity? Of course, the wellbeing of those who interact rises if, beyond salary, such activity is exercised with kindness. The salary can surely be an excellent reason to work but, even within this simple motivation, there can still be some free space left for gratuity (at least in the way we understand it).

We are certainly more satisfied when we find in our market partners a "surplus" of motivations, but it is also possible to have a truly civil experience operating in a joint activity with them when we are fair, non-opportunistic and we nourish sentiments of mutual friendship. The message that these pages try to transmit is a non-ideological and pluralistic vision of human motivations: organizations, including VBOs, are and have to be plural and pluralistic places also in terms of their member's motivations. That is why, from one point of view, it would not be particularly clever and fruitful to disregard the ones who work just in order to maintain themselves and their families without having any particular intrinsic motivation; aside from this, to investigate our colleagues and collaborators in order to classify, hire and fire the individuals according to the valuation of the grade of their intrinsic motivation, would be one really dangerous and particularly illiberal practice. The economy and the organizations function well when the management and the different levels of responsibility, conscious that people's motivations are different, stop on the edge of individuals' privacy and manage to create synergy between the diversities (also the motivational ones) without creating competitive and conflict dynamics among them.

In this chapter, we have tried to show that between the possibility to conceive work as self-sacrifice vs. pure individualistic self-self-interest and "mutual indifference," there can be a third way. This is one of Civil Economy tradition, where market is by its nature based on mutual advantages and assistance, as an important dimension of the life of civil society. Markets and economy are also pieces of our life in common which become civil or uncivil depending on how we see and live them, on our intentions, feelings and actions. Reciprocity, in its various forms, is the law both of civil society and of the market.

If we continue, instead, to read the economic life as a sphere separated from the civil one, in accordance to the tradition of western thought (defined by some radical dichotomies such as soul-body, eros-*agape*, faith-reason, gift-market), then we will leave the high passions and ideals on the coat rack of our factories and offices since they are not "insiders" and thus "they do not have access to the sites of economic and civil life." But such a dualistic and Manichean interpretation of life continues simply to generate a twofold error: from one side, it contributes to keep ideals distant from economic behaviour, with consequences that we can all observe in the markets today, too often dull and lacking in good/happy passions (but full of sad ones); from the other, it holds the economic values and the virtues of the market (efficiency, responsibility, scarcity) outside those fields governed by ideal motivations. This leads to a sort of isolation and thus inefficiency in order to defend VBOs from the cynical and devoid-of-ideals market, which is itself reduced by a lack of high passions and ideals in its own arena.

We are convinced, in fact, that the dichotomic way of thinking gift-market and economy-ideals, which is the fruit of some great cultural traumas in the early modern age, is one of the main obstacles to overcome towards achieving true humanization of the market today. We believe that this dichotomy of market-ideals has to be overcome for the good of VBOs and of ideals, and for the good of the economy in general.

Until now we have not often met in the world of ideals and values a proper relationship with the economic field: on some occasions it has been enslaved to serve it and in others, most of the times indeed, it has been rendered tyrannical. Banks and entrepreneurs are considered ambiguous figures but whose money is needed, so they often become masters of many VBOs, inside and outside the religions, that are not able to contact with the economic world in a climate of mutual esteem and respect. We are still waiting for the age of fraternity, in which the economy would be neither a servant nor a master, but a "sister."

In the following chapters, we will get to the heart of our argument, starting in Chapter 3 with an attempt to give a definition of VBOs and to go deeper into some of their dynamics such as the process of selection of new members or of managing crises, especially those concerning the quality of ideals.

Notes

1 On the topic of relational goods see Gui (2002) and Gui-Sugden (2005).
2 Whoever today wants to refer an ethical critic to the market cannot avoid taking into consideration its civilizing and social function, which can be lost in an attempt to establish an economy based on the "gift exchange" erasing in this way centuries of civilization and which made it possible for the market to be formed/appear and develop. That is why every serious and civil critic of the market has to recognize at least such moral function and orient its critical evaluation so as not to contradict this dimension of market interactions—such as a certain communitarianist philosophy is doing today. All these considerations were well known to the civil tradition of economics, which is our starting point in imagining caring relationships that express fraternity, without renouncing the market.
3 It would be enough to think about the social costs related to disadvantaged and not included people.
4 It is necessary to be reminded that every person has his/her own "daimon" which should be released in order to fulfill his/her excellence; also a young person with Down syndrome has his/her own path towards excellence and has to discover and let flourish his own "daimon."
5 We believe that the world of the elderly represents today a new border where it is possible to grasp these occasions of mutual advantage.

3 The art of gratuity

And here it is the idea of this work. If we were to fix our eyes on such nice and useful truths, we would not study either because of a dull vanity, or because of our desire to dominate the illiterate, and cruelly ignore them, but in order to respect the laws of the moderator of this world, which commands us to learn how to be one useful to the others.

(Antonio Genovesi 1765)

Motivations and economic life

The motivations underlying our actions have an important value in life, in its civil and economic dimensions as well as in organizations. Human beings are the sole animals able to attribute meaning and value not only to the material payoffs deriving from certain kinds of behavior, but also to their own motivations and those of others as well. Motivations (including the ones which are more complex than the simple pursuit of profit) will matter till as long as organizations and markets remain "human places" (Bruni-Zamagni 2012).

Motivations underlying human actions are not seen, or at least had not been seen until recent times, to have particular interest to economics. For non-banal reasons, the modern economic science considers it quite dangerous to include them in its analysis, since its main and maybe most ingrained characteristic is the definition of the market as a field in which people can meet and exchange without taking into account "why" each agent is driven to perform a certain activity or exchange. The analysis of these "whys" regards the identities, personal stories, classes, religions—all elements that during the ancient regime (and to a certain point still in many parts of the world today) have served as a limitation to the economic and social development and have confined human interactions to the field of strong clan, group and family relations, to the parental and friendship networks.

It is exactly the capacity of the market to create a new system of human relations, a new ethos, that stops on the threshold of individual *motivations* and contends with the laic and anonymous *choices* which people make, that has stood as the basis of its extraordinary development during the centuries. When we go to buy a bottle of wine in the supermarket nobody asks us why we are about to make such a purchase (either for a party with our friends or in order to satisfy our desire for alcohol): for the market mechanism it is enough that whoever buys has got the purchasing power to do so and follows the price signals of the market. We are not asked by the shopkeeper in the supermarket[1] whether we are Muslims, Jews or Christians: the market interaction goes beyond such diversities, it is indifferent to people's different motivations. For this same reason, the analysis of motivations is always delicate/tricky since the investigation of motivations in public life and in the world of work should not become an instrument of discrimination and control of human beings.

It is exactly because the market stops on the threshold of motivations that it can operate a sort of *leveling of the identities*: because of their extraordinary capacity to make possible the encounter of human beings that would have never met if the market interaction had been dependent on motivations and, thus, on identities, the market relations have managed to include billions of people who had previously remained for thousands of years on the edge of public life and have activated people's desire to live and grow (even when consumer goods are not the best answer to the will of life and growth of human beings).

The eminent English economist P. Wicksteed, an Unitarian theologian and Dante scholar, is the one who has mainly theorized such characteristics of modern economics as he stated that in regard to actions economists had to be "concerned with the 'what' and the 'how', and not at all in 'why'" (Wicksteed 1933[1910] p. 165); in this way, actions remain free from any analysis of the motives: "the things and doings with which economic investigation is concerned will therefore be found to include ... the things a man can give to or for another independently of any personal and individualized sympathy with him or with his motives or reasons" (ibid., pp. 4–5).

From this point of view, however, thanks also to the progress of the dialogue between economics and psychology and the consequent growing use of the experimental method in economics, in the last decades economic scholars have realized that motivations have some important effects on the choices made by people and on those who observe the act of making such choices. It has been experimentally discovered (in addition to the observation of people's real life) that if we did not insert motivations in the economic analysis, we would not be able to understand many important choices (such as the act of trust, the positive or negative response to it, the act of paying back such trust, of choosing a certain job and engaging in it, of paying the taxes, complying with laws, etc.): all of them are dependent on the way in which individuals read and interpret the motivations of the ones with whom they interact.[2]

What are VBOs?

This recent opening in economics of the subject of motivations is important since the dynamics of VBOs can be studied and understood only within an economic science that takes motivations into account. If there was, indeed, a place in which motivations play a special role, it would be a VBO: an expression that starts to be used today in regard to those organizations—associations, NGOs, social enterprises, economy of communion companies, etc.—whose guiding principle (at least at the stage of their foundation) is neither profit, nor some strictly material elements, but an ideal motivation, a mission or "vocation" which is related in different ways to the intrinsic motivations of those who promote it. And when it comes to mission, to intrinsic motivations, to vocation, gratuity is also concerned if it is true—and this is our hypothesis—that we enter the field of gratuity every time we have to deal with some kind of behavior which is put into practice because it is good, because of its intrinsic value, before and independently (at least in the short term[3]) of its material results.

In the economic and social literature, there is no shared definition of VBOs and they are normally identified with religious organizations.[4] The ideal motivation of such organizations may take various forms: it can be found in the kind of activity they perform, in the motivations that stand as the basis of their foundation (for example, in the case of an enterprise founded in order to include the most disadvantaged individuals in the productive process), or in the way of doing business that concerns the choice of governance or organizational structure. According to us, these characteristics have to be co-present in a VBO, even though in different degrees and combinations, since it is difficult to imagine, for example, an ideal motivation that does not combine with an adequate governance or organizational structure, as the "new wine" of the ideal mission normally needs "new wineskins" in which it can mature over time.

In this book the term VBO will be applied to any organization that exhibits three basic elements: one related to the organization and two to its members:

- The activity carried out in the organization is an essential part of its identity, because the VBO objects are engendered by a "vocation" that represents the values, the identity and the mission of the organization.[5] If the owners of a capitalistic company could easily change the field of activity when convenient, a VBO is created with a specific aim/objective which is inextricably linked to the organization. In other words, in a VBO the activity performed cannot be practically or logically separated from the desired result. The activity, therefore, is a constitutive part of the objective to which it is oriented.

- The identity of the organization is an essential element, although, as with every identity, it is one dynamic reality in continuous co-evolution together with environment and history. It is deeply linked to a core of members who share, and in a certain sense embody the "vocation" and the ethical values of the VBO.[6] We will call these members, who are often (but not necessarily) the founders of the VBO, intrinsically motivated individuals. To say "vocation" means, in our account, to recognize that in these core members *gratuity* (in the terms that we are about to define) is at work.[7]
- These intrinsically motivated "core members" are less reactive to price signals (i.e. wage) as compared with other less intrinsically motivated members, and are most reactive to the ideal quality of the VBO and thus the first to protest. The core members are the "guardians" of the identity and ideal quality of the VBO, therefore they are the most ready to signal an alarm, i.e. "voice," should a deterioration of that ideal quality and value occur.

In order to understand VBO's peculiarities, it can be useful to think about what a VBO is not: organizations, for example, whose only purpose is to maximize profit, or organizations in which the activity is just instrumental to optimizing something else, and where the employees react only to wage and material incentives and no particular "vocation" (apart from technical skills and the respect of the contract) is requested from its members.

Examples of VBOs include non-profit organizations, charities, NGOs, environmental, educational or cultural organizations.[8]

The main objective of any VBO is to evolve and grow without losing its identity, on which its survival depends in the middle and long run.[9] As a matter of fact, if on one hand an organization "cannot survive if not tending towards progress, which is always qualitative but very often also one dimensional … since without tension towards progress normally there is no stability, but regression" (Molteni 2009, p. 72), on the other, such progress has to be reconciled with loyalty to the ideal mission which means dynamic loyalty to the identity of the organization.

Anyone operating in the field of social economy or organizations characterized by a mission that goes beyond profits knows very well that in such organizations the success and harmonious growth of the organization chiefly depends on a few key persons (often, as said, some of the founders of the organization) who are intrinsically motivated. These core members directly affect (through governance choices, rules, etc.) the culture of the organization and, most importantly in our analysis, indirectly through their actions that are imitated by others, less intrinsically motivated members. Once some of these core members leave the organizations (because, for example, new management does not completely buy into the ideal of the founder), cumulative effects often occur and a huge deterioration process may start within the organization. One important remedy against this deterioration process is the loyalty of the core members, which can be fostered by a participative and pluralistic governance.

The ideal type of VBO we have in mind could be a primary school founded and run by a congregation of nuns (i.e. a typical case in VBO literature) that intends to continue the activity only if the core teachers (the nuns) see the ideal quality of the school in line with their spirituality. Another example of a VBO is an environmental NGO born from a small group of people who are trying to protect an endangered species of bird. When the NGO grows, the key issue is to keep the original "vocation," from which the NGO began, embodied especially in the culture of the core intrinsically motivated founding members.

At the start of this chapter we said that gratuity played an essential role inside the VBO. But what is gratuity? It is not the *tip*, as understood, not by chance, in the US.[10] In the next paragraph we will try to define some of its characteristics.

What is gratuity?

Life in common would be unthinkable if there were no behaviors inspired by gratuity because without gratuity there is not any fully human encounter and no sincere trust can be generated. And if such trust is lacking, neither organizations, nor the market and society can function. If we were to erase, indeed, gratuity from ordinary economic matters, our productive organizations and most of our markets would implode over a morning.

Since gratuity is a fundamental dimension of what we call "human" and, thus, it exceeds the sole economic dimension, it is extremely difficult to define it, in particular in its socio-economic declinations. Such difficulty can explain why we cannot find any integrated reflection on gratuity in social literature, especially in the economic one. We meet more and more words that are semantically close to it, such as gift, reciprocity, philanthropy, etc. but gratuity still remains undefined.

When the dimension of gratuity is activated, the way to go has the same importance as the goal to achieve. The action has to have an intrinsic value and not just an instrumental one. Pure non-instrumentality or intrinsic motivations, though, are only one necessary but not sufficient condition in order to talk about gratuity and about human behaviors inspired by it (only what is "human" knows what gratuity is). The ancient category which tells us what gratuity is, is *agape* since there is no behavior inspired by it which lacks gratuity. This necessary condition serves to distinguish gratuity from altruism or from philanthropy, which can also be experiences lacking in intrinsic motivations. Gifts can certainly be an expression of gratuity, but in its dimension can also prevail the duty related to the ancient *munus*. A word that captures this "necessary" dimension of gratuity is the one that we find mostly in children, the *innocence*: a child who plays without any other particular goal than the game in itself expresses this dimension of gratuity.

The intentional orientation of the action towards good even if such good is not necessarily "the good of the other" is the sufficient condition to talk about gratuity. Such condition can exclude from the category of gratuity the child who plays: it is not enough to be a child in order to experience gratuity but if we want to experience real gratuity, it is necessary to restore the childish dimension also when adults.

Even in the most "regular" behaviors within the market there is the need of something that the contract—also because of its incompleteness—cannot predict. And it is needed during the ordinary course of economic affairs, while we produce, work and exchange, and not only after as a "surplus" that often ends up being confused with the superfluous and useless, something similar to the *limoncello* (liqueur) served after the meal—cute but not necessary.

But how can we put together—if it is possible—relational goods (which require gratuity) and normal economic transactions? As we have mentioned in the last chapter, it is well-known for those who deal with such issues, that if I were paid to smile at an old person, my smile could lose its immaterial but extremely real nature which was exactly what the client desired; or if I were taught to be kind and pay attention to the customers in order to sell more, exactly the opposite effect to the one desired can occur right after the client notices the instrumentality of my behavior. That does not mean that we deny the importance of requiring nurses, doctors, officials, bartenders to treat customers and citizens politely: this is a sign of civilization. Therefore, gratuity is different from kindness and good education, or from political correctness (even if it does not exclude them).

In order to understand what value gratuity has, it is enough to think that it is exactly the fact that friendship, love, prayer and beauty are essentially acts of gratuity, which makes them the most precious goods in our life. As a matter of fact, if we think of it for a moment, it is gratuity which makes the difference between a "true" friend and an "opportunistic" one, between the relationships within a family and the exchange of goods and services, between a work of art and any other commodity, between prayer and witchcraft or superstition. Therefore, all of us know what place gratuity has in our concrete life experience, all of us look for it and, above all, suffer in the cases in which we miss it in ourselves, in others, or when it has been betrayed. However, if we try to think about it, to understand and define it, it seems as if it slips away, that it becomes either too complex or even banal. And it is maybe better to leave it undefined, or define it only in the negative indicating what gratuity is not.

We might also say that the great strength of VBOs lies in their ability to give value to gratuity: founded on the basis of vocation, such organizations have the specific taste of gratuity since probably only things that express an interior vocation can be truly gratuitous because they are truly free. Only where there is freedom, indeed, there can be also gratuity, and only gratuity is truly free because it allows us to act moved from the inside, obeying in such a way our Socratic *daimon* and, thus, our deepest nature, the best part of ourselves.

Therefore, gratuity is one of those "profound" words such as beauty, love, truth, freedom or communion, which are, at the same time, particular and universal. These words have in common the characteristic that each of them also contains the others: a good life does not consist of beauty, truth, or freedom separately, but of all of them together. Each of these words shows the essence of the good life.

Modern culture has tried to confine gratuity to the private sphere, expelling it definitely from the public one. In particular, from the economic field in which taking into account contracts, incentives, good rules and interests seems to be enough. But the process of losing contact with the territory of gratuity can open the way to the implosion of economic activities, and it is what we observe more and more clearly in the economy today.

The straight wall

Gratuity should not be seen just as the contents of human action. The gift-gratuity is, instead, mainly the act of giving oneself away, the act of being and receiving, the silence that comes before the word. That is why the action moved by gratuity may take various forms since gratuity is a mode of it, it is "how" we act. In our opinion, this is the truest meaning of gift-gratuity and what makes it possible and necessary to notice it within the process of carrying out any kind of human action and, thus, even when we do our duty, fulfill a contract, operate in the market, or in the company.

Therefore, the "gift" that results from gratuity is not the same as the gadget, the discount, the present, the points accumulated on our fidelity cards which are all expressions of this kind of "gift" normally practiced in the market that in general do not have anything to do with true gratuity and with its tragic and painful nature. True gratuity, in fact, places me in front of the other without any mediator, it renders me fragile because it exceeds the calculation of equivalences as well as the contractual and legal warranties. True gratuity is always a potential wound. And as a result of its tragic nature modernity has expelled it from the markets, from the economy and from the public sphere in general.

We can find an example of *such* gratuity in the works of two authors that, even though quite different from the other, are united by the strong sorrow experienced (in fact, sorrow is a great school of gratuity when it does not turn into desperation): Primo Levi and Pavel A. Florenskij. Recalling his experience in the concentration camp, Primo Levi wrote:

> I have often noticed in Auschwitz one curious phenomenon: the need of the work "well done" that is ingrained in man and drives him to do well even the imposed, slave labour. The Italian bricklayer who saved my life by secretly bringing me food over six months, used to hate the Nazi, their food, their language, their war: but when they made him build walls, he used to build them straight and solid, not because of obedience but because of dignity.
>
> (Levi 1997, p. 85)

Building a "straight wall" because of dignity is also an expression of gratuity because it shows us that in ourselves, in others, in nature, in things, and even in walls, there is a "truth" and a "vocation" that has to be respected and served, and never "enslaved" by our interests. "That wall was himself" commented during a conference near Forli a lute musician and humanist named Foscolo. "The bricklayer had embodied in that wall the beauty and strength which he was not able to see in himself anymore in such inhuman living conditions. Just like saying: "Even if all of you see something different, in reality I am like this wall: nice and straight." Only an artist, someone who brings the *daimon* of the vocation that is always a question of gratuity, could possibly make such a comment about this passage.

Gratuity can also become an art, *the art of gratuity* as the eminent Russian theologian and scientist Pavel Florenskij had defined a few months before he was shot dead in the *gulag* of Solovki:

> Things in my life have always happened like this. In the same moment in which I used to gain the knowledge of a certain subject, I was also forced to leave it for reasons beyond my will and to face a new problem, starting always from its bases in order to pave the way for others, not me. There is maybe a deep meaning hidden in this situation, since it repeats itself during the entire human life: *the art of gratuity*.
>
> (Florenskij 2009, pp. 397–8)

The economic affairs marked by this kind of gratuity are important attempts to give value to the civilizing and liberating function of the market without declining the use of gratuity with its tragic nature. In such situations there is always a vital tension between the "wounds" and the "blessings": those who found a social cooperative, a Fair Trade shop or an Economy of Communion company may live happier but, at the same time, suffer more because in the encounter with the other, which is always "tragic" but also full of surprises, there is no way to escape and hide in the immunizing hierarchy or in the contract (aspects that we will examine further).

If gratuity and gift really are as we have tried to define them, there is no need to "leave" the economic field and "enter" into the social one each time they come close to the field of economic interactions. If the openness to gratuity characterizes the truly human dimension, and if economy is a human activity, one truly human economy, then, we cannot leave aside gratuity, since in this way we would find ourselves out of both what we can define human and economic. Therefore, if the economic activities are "human," they cannot ever be ethically and anthropologically neutral: economy either builds relationships based on justice and *charitas* or destroys them: *tertium non datur*.

From such a perspective, the market is called back to its original but too often betrayed vocation as a factor of social inclusion (which can be found also in Adam Smith's work and not only in Genovesi's and in the Italian tradition of Civil Economy) in which the contract is subsidiary and not a substitute for the authentic human promotion and for the common good.

It is also thanks to *such* gratuity that VBOs live—or most of them.[11] The main objective of a VBO is to grow and develop without losing the loyalty to its ideal motivation, without detaching from its charisma, therefore, without losing its gratuity dimension (*charis*).

This gratuity is, therefore, deeply attached to what we call *agape* (although they are not synonymous, given the ages that separate the two deeply related concepts), to the *caritas* which in the first centuries of Christian history was written also *charitas* in order to enhance it being the translation of both *agape* (love) and *charis* (gratuity).

Agape: an old name for gratuity

Reciprocity is the golden rule of human sociality. Only the word reciprocity can explain the basic structure of society, even if that society is characterized by indignation, revenge and endless court cases. The DNA of the political being is a twisting helix of giving and receiving. Even human love is essentially a matter of reciprocity from its first moment to its last. Just think of how often someone departs from this earth holding the hand of their beloved or, in their absence, clasping it in their thoughts with the last strength of their mind and heart. Reciprocity is the dimension of love where we love those who love us; there have been many ways and many words to express this in different human cultures.

In ancient Greek culture, the most common ways of expressing love were *eros* and, although with a specific and less universalistic meaning, *philia*. These were two different forms of love, but they have one thing in common: reciprocity, the basic need for a response from the other. *Eros* is direct reciprocity, which is two-way and exclusive; it is where the other is loved because it fills a need and because love satisfies us. It is revived again and again, a vital desire. In the Greek idea of *philia* (which is similar, not identical, to what we now call friendship), reciprocity is more complex. In *philia* relationships, a lack of response from the other is tolerated, giving and receiving are not always kept in balance and forgiveness is possible/ necessary many times. That's why *eros* is not a virtue, but *philia* can be because it requires loyalty, even from a friend that temporarily betrays us and does not return our love. But the *philia* type of love is not unconditional love as it is cut off when the other—by not returning my feelings—makes me realize that he or she no longer wants to be my friend.

Eros and *philia* are wonderful and essential for good life, yet, they are not enough. A human is great precisely because the existing greatness of reciprocity is not enough for us; we want the infinite. So, at some point in history, when the right time came, the need arose to find another word for a dimension of love that is not contained in those two words for love, no matter how rich and elevated they both were. This new word, *agape,* was not entirely new to Greek vocabulary, but its use and meaning were new. It was used to characterise the people that were commonly called "those of the road," the first name of Christians. *Agape* was not an invention, but it was a revelation of a dimension of power that is present inside every person, even when it remains buried and is waiting for someone to say "come out." It is not a form of love that begins where the other forms end, and it is not the opposite of either *eros* or *philia* because *agape* is what makes every love complete and mature. For it is *agape* that gives love the human dimension of graciousness that is not guaranteed by *philia* and, even less so, *eros*. By opening them up, it makes way for the fulfilment of the virtues that without it are subtly selfish. For the same reason, they chose *charitas* when *agape* was translated to Latin, which in earlier times was spelled with the "h" in it, a very rarely used letter. Its insertion into the word changed everything because it could mean many things.

The first message was that *charitas* was neither *amor* (love) nor *amicitia* (friendship), but it was something else. Furthermore, this *charitas* was no longer the *caritas* of Roman merchants, who used it to express the value of goods (those that cost a lot are "caro"). But that letter "h" also served to remind everyone that *charitas* pointed to another great Greek word: *charis*, grace or gracefulness. There is no *agape* without *charis*, and there is no *charis* without *agape*. While *philia* can forgive up to seven times, *agape* will until seventy times seven; *philia* gives the tunic but *agape* gives the cloak too, and *philia* walks a mile with his friend but *agape* walks two and not only with friends. *Eros* endures, hopes and covers little; *philia* covers, endures, hopes a lot; *agape* hopes, covers and endures all.

The form that *agape* love takes provides great power for action, economic and social change. Every time a person acts for good, finding the resources for it in the action itself and inside themselves even without the promise of reciprocity, is when *agape* is at work. *Agape* is the love that is typical of founders who start a new movement, or an NGO, without being able to count on the reciprocity of others. They are the ones that act with the fortitude and perseverance necessary to endure the long periods of loneliness. *Agape* does not affect the choice to "love back" the other, but when unrequited it suffers; *agape* is only complete with reciprocity, but it does not hurt so much as to cut off its love if it remains unrequited. It is, the agapic one, a special kind of reciprocity, that we call "unconditional reciprocity"— a special kind, but unlike what scholars like Luc Boltanski think, the Agapic relationship remains a form of reciprocity, because is affected by the not-reprocity of the others (Bruni 2008).

The fullness of reciprocity in *agape* is also expressed in a ternary relationship: A gives himself to B, and B gives himself to C—*agape* is transitive unlike *philia* and *eros*. Indeed, this dimension of "impartiality" and openness is essential to bring about *agape*.

Even the maternal and paternal love for a child would not be *agape*, so mature and complete, if it were spent in the relation A=>B, B=>A, without the dimension B=>C, which overcomes every temptation of incestuous or narcissistic love.

The need for reciprocity and to keep going even when there is no answer is what makes *agape* a relational experience, which is at once vulnerable and fertile. *Agape* is a most fertile wound. It is *agape* that shapes our communities into welcoming and inclusive places with doors wide open that never close. This is what undermines sacred hierarchies, caste systems, and the temptation of power. Furthermore, *agape* is essential for every common good because it knows the kind of forgiveness that is able to undo the wrongs done to us. Anyone who has been the victim of evil, of any evil, will know that the evil done and received cannot be fully compensated for or repaired by penalties and paying for damages. It lives on like a wound that is still there. This is the case unless one day it meets the forgiveness of *agape*, which, unlike the forgiveness of *eros* and *philia*, is able to heal all wounds, even the mortal ones, making them the dawn of a resurrection.

However, there is a theory that has been present throughout the history of our culture. *Agape*—they say—cannot be a civil form of love; to allow such vulnerability would not be prudent. It can only be lived in family life, spiritual life and perhaps in volunteering. In the streets and businesses, however, we should be contented with the different ranges of *eros* (incentives) and, at most, of *philia*. This thesis is deeply rooted because, at least partly, it is based on historical evidence of the many experiences born of *agape*—we return to hierarchy or communitarianism. It is the story of many communities—including VBOs—that started with *agape* and, upon receiving the first wounds, end up transforming themselves into very hierarchical and formal systems. It is also the story of experiences that were born to be open and inclusive but, after their first failures, closed their doors, expelling all that was different. History is also a succession of these instances of "stepping back," but these instances do not reduce the civil value of *agape*. On the contrary, they should motivate us to put more *agape* (and not less) into politics, business and work. For every time that *agape* makes an appearance in human history, even if it stays just for a short or very short time, it never leaves the world unchanged. The body heat has risen again and again, and a new nail is driven into the rock; the starting point of those who begin their climb tomorrow will be a few meters or, at least, centimeters higher. Not a drop of *agape* is wasted on the earth. *Agape* broadens the horizon of possibilities for the good of humanity; it is the yeast and salt of every good bread. The world does not die, and life begins again every morning because there are people capable of *agape*: "*And now these three remain: faith, hope and agape. But the greatest of these is agape*" (1 Corinthians, 13).

After this (maybe necessary) digression, in the next chapters we will examine some of the dynamics characterizing the process of development of VBOs and, in particular, some specific points of the difficult process of selection of personnel and of governance in times when motivational and ideal crises occur.

Notes

1 The mechanism in more relationship-sensitive and communitarian markets in real cities where such questions are actually made, is actually different.
2 For a review and an experiment on the nature of motivations in contemporary economics see Stanca-Bruni-Corazzini (2009).
3 On the possibility that intrinsic motivations change in time see Bruni (2006. Chapter 5).
4 Mitroff-Denton (1999) have identified five models of a VBO and all of them are based on religious and spiritual nature.
5 "Activity" here should be understood in a broad sense. In the case of a social cooperative, for example, the concrete activities performed can be different and can change in time (laundry, assembly, etc.) but we see as "activity" the work rehabilitation of disadvantaged workers which is the one that constitutes the mission of the VBO. In other cases (as in charities, for example) the relationship between mission and activity is even stronger.

The art of gratuity 43

6 We use here the terms "vocation," "ideal motivation," and "intrinsic motivation" synonymously. In fact, between ideal motivation or vocation and intrinsic motivation there is a very strict link. There is no ideal motivation without intrinsic motivation for the activity engendered.

7 This means that the presence of the dimension of gratuity—via, at least, its core members—is an essential element of VBOs.

8 It is easy to understand that not all non-profit or civil society organizations are VBOs.

9 In this broader sense, many organizations can be included in the VBO category. This list can include, for example, small, family-based for-profit firms whose development and survival are seriously challenged after the first generation of founders (which is occurring nowadays in the Italian districts comprised of "Made in Italy" brands). Once the first generation retires, these small firms tend to encounter huge difficulties finding new managers within the market who are able to preserve the identity and business culture imbued by the entrepreneur. This specific and people-based culture represents the main competitive power of such firms, embodying the tacit know-how of the entrepreneurs.

10 It is interesting to notice how much languages embody semantic and cultural differences in words. Not only is the only understandable meaning of gratuity a tip in the U.S., but the Latin word *charitas*—very similar to what we now call gratuity in Latin countries—became charity, that is one main institution of the philanthropic capitalism of the protestant matrix.

11 In this book, we treat all VBOs as a unique type or category. But, as in every theoretical (ideal-typical) analysis, the reality is variagated and various. Not all real or actual VBOs, for instance, have *agape* among their explicit founding principles and values—although without some form of *agape*/gratuity it is hard to imagine a "true" VBO—we can play with the ambiguity of these rich words.

4   When vocation matters

> For know that this is the command necessity of God; and I believe that no greater good has ever happened in the state than my service to the God.
>
> (*Apology of Socrates*)

How to hire Socrates?

In every single organization, recruitment is one extremely delicate process. The ability to attract the right people is a crucial element of the balanced and harmonious growth in time of VBOs, founded on the basis of a clear *mission*. The challenges related to the process of recruitment become particularly tricky in the moments in which dimensional growth or intergenerational change in VBOs occur.

As a matter of fact, the need to substitute some of their core members, makes the intergenerational change one critical moment in the life of VBOs. The stage of selection of new members is a physiological dimension of each organization whose existence lasts longer than the lifetime of its founders.

In this chapter, we will analyze the phenomenon of recruitment of new members (such as shareholders, employees or managers) within VBOs. Such organizations are particularly interested in attracting people (at least a certain number of them) who have the "vocation" to perform the specific kind of activity in which the organization's *mission* consists. Every VBO needs someone who teaches, who cures the ill or deals with the growth of the poor, driven by vocation and not only by wage. In the same way, unlike the Sophists in Athens, Socrates did not accept payments for his lectures. At the same time, we have to admit that modern Socrates need their wages to live. We need, therefore, to think of a specific kind of governance of incentives which manages to attract "Socrates" (or at least some of them).

We will see that it is not necessary that all the members of a VBO are intrinsically motivated (have a "vocation") so that a good climate and cooperation can be established within the organization. However, it is necessary that intrinsic motivations are the driving force of at least a *certain number* of them. When they reach a critical mass, these men become able to move others, although lacking in strong intrinsic motivations, to behave in a cooperative way also. Vocation and intrinsic motivation are, in fact, two sides of the same coin.

We begin this chapter with a brief introduction to the standard theory of personnel selection, as seen in economics. We consider an ordinary real-life situation when there is incomplete and asymmetric information between the individual applying for a job and the VBO which has to select him. We will see afterwards, in the central part of the chapter, several models proposing alternative theories in case we have to deal with organizations interested in the presence of a true "vocation" in the workers they hire. Such models, that we have already mentioned, are based on the idea that a good instrument of "vocation" selection could be a wage offer lower than the one practiced in the market ("to pay less"). We will conclude this chapter by making our own suggestion: to fill in some of the gaps of the present theory by proposing a non-conventional interpretation of the nature and role of vocation in VBOs.

Our initial hypothesis consists of supposing that the managers of a VBO are interested in selecting workers who have "vocation." They are, thus, interested in hiring not just prepared and capable individuals, but ones who, even though prepared,[1] feel the *mission* and values of the organization as if they were their own. Along the lines of what is suggested nowadays, we call this a surplus "vocation." In order to give an example right away, let us consider a social cooperative which deals with the integration of disadvantaged people in the workforce. It does not, therefore, want to select only technically prepared managers and employees,[2] but desires, or should desire, that beyond their technical preparedness, there is also a certain dose of "vocation," of interest, of passion (of *timos*, as Plato would say), of intrinsic motivations for the activity or mission they are going to perform.

In the language introduced in the previous chapter, we can say that a VBO would like to select workers who are *capable of gratuity* while carrying out their work—in the ordinary work, not only in the (free and not paid) extra-work. Such vocation should lead workers to approach the disadvantaged men with care and attention which no contract could ever guarantee or enforce with sanctions and incentives. As a matter of fact, the success and survival within time of VBOs often depends on the fact that clients and various stakeholders look for and recognize in these organizations the specific "surplus" they probably do not see in a public structure or in a *for-profit* company. What can we do, then, in order to attract to VBOs prepared workers who *also* have vocation?

The first theoretical element of our analysis of this complex issue is one of the most influential papers in economics in the past decades. We refer to a paper that has changed great parts of the way in which economic relations are seen (and economic books are written): "The market of lemons" from George Akerlof, published in 1970. The basic idea of this short essay (that earned its author the Nobel prize for economics), is an application of one of the oldest economic theories, the so called "Gresham's law" which states: *Bad money drives out good.* Gresham's law refers to a phenomenon very common mostly in societies of the ancient regime which occurs whenever a territory circulates money with different intrinsic values but with the same liberating power. In such cases the money considered less good (the "bad" notes) circulate more rapidly (since everyone wants to get rid of them). Therefore, soon the "good" money disappears (because kept and treasured secretly at home).[3]

Nowadays, thanks also to Akerlof, we know that this law has a general application and concerns not only money but a vast area of economic and social phenomena, of relational and motivational kinds, as well.

In his work, Akerlof has gone to the roots of Gresham's law. He has demonstrated that the reason why the market mechanism selects the bad rather than the good money is due essentially to an *information* problem. It consists of an *asymmetric information* exchange between the contracting parties: one party (which offers money in exchange for commodities) knows something more than the other. He is aware if money he is about to use in the contract is good or bad. At the same time the other party (which receives the money) knows less, since it is not able to distinguish good from bad money.[4]

The example used by Akerlof in his paper—an example that we can find today in every textbook of economics—concerns the functioning of the used car market. We quote it here because we believe that it would facilitate our comprehension of VBOs and of the process of recruitment of men with a certain degree of "vocation."

Let us suppose that there are two types of used cars on the market: "good" quality and "bad" quality ones (called *lemons*). Anyone who wants to sell a car on the market is aware whether the car he offers is a good one or a lemon (the seller knows, for example, whether the car has a defect which is hard to detect during a test drive or at a glance: a noise in the bodywork or a defect in the air conditioning that comes out only in certain circumstances). The buyer, instead, cannot directly observe and verify when signing the contract. Because of this informational imperfection the buyer sets the price of the car on the basis of an estimate. In such cases the most ordinary way of estimating the value of the car is based on its *expected value*. If, for example, the price on the market of one "good" used car is 4,000 euros, the price of a "bad" one is 2,000 euros and the probability to find a good car is 50 percent (0.5), the expected value which the agent offers to the seller is the following:

$$P = 4,000 \ (0.5) + 2,000 \ (0.5) = 3,000$$

Therefore, if the buyer uses this estimate in the presence of imperfect information, he will offer 3,000 euros for any kind of used car, not being able to distinguish at this stage the good ones from the lemons.

How, then, will the used car market function? It is easy to guess that its bad functioning and failure will occur. In fact, those who are aware that they own a good car will not accept the price offer of 3,000 euros since it is less than 4,000 (which is the minimum price these owners are ready to accept in exchange for the good cars they offer). On the contrary, those who know they own a lemon will offer their cars right away since at a price of 3,000 they gain 1,000 euro of net profit [the market price (3,000) minus the real value of the car (2,000)]. Here are the immediate conclusions of Akerlof's reflection, that reveal several problematic and interesting aspects:

- First, those who own a good car will not manage to sell it (except where they accept a price lower than the real value of the car, making in this way an economically inefficient exchange).
- Second, there soon will be only bad used cars placed on the used car market since they will be the ones selected.
- Third, those looking for a good used car will not do it on this market since, if they think rationally, they will realize that it is crowded only with lemons.
- Last, the fact that you are trying to sell an used car will be interpreted from one rational buyer as a *signal* that this car is a lemon.

An asymmetric information problem underlies the failure of the used car market. Even if there were both potential sellers of good cars and some potential buyers (even at a price higher than 3,000 euros on the market), they would never meet.[5]

Akerlof's results have been applied to a great number of different situations: from the case of wedding agencies (the fact that you subscribe to a wedding agency "signals" that you are a person whose esthetic and relational quality is lower than the average); to the insurance companies (how is it possible to avoid that only the less prudent individuals take out theft insurance, or that mostly the seriously ill take out life insurance?) and the credit on the labor market,[6] which we analyze here. If during the process of recruitment the company does not recognize the ability and will to work of the person it intends to hire, it will offer a wage of 300 (on the basis of the estimate of the expected value. A "good" worker's pay-off for the company would be 400, while a "bad" one's—less prepared or willing—only 200), Akerlof's theory tells us that, at this wage rate, only "bad" workers will apply for the job.

Obviously, such a result is not a good message for economics. As a matter of fact, companies often manage to also hire (although not only) prepared and willing workers. Therefore, it seems that the most significant failure which Akerlof's model shows us, is the failure of standard economic theory, which had been based up to the 70s on some extremely simplified hypotheses that made it really difficult to comprehend the real-life economic and social dynamics.

After Akerlof, indeed, new solutions or remedies for such failures due to asymmetric information problems (failures of the theory rather than the market itself, we repeat) have been sought in economics. Such remedies can be divided into two big families: those based on *supply* (for example, a worker who offers his work, a seller who offers his used car, etc.) and those based on *demand* (for example, a company demanding work, a buyer looking for an used car, etc.). The solution proposed by models based on supply consists in a "signal" that the offering party gives to the other party in order to reveal his higher than the average quality. Some typical examples are: the role of education on the labor market (for a company, the fact that one worker has a bachelor's degree can be a signal that he is better and deserves a higher wage than a worker who does not have it); the "guarantee" on the used car market which signals, in an expensive (and, thus, credible) way, that one car's quality is higher than the average (and therefore the buyer from our previous example, could pay a price higher than 3,000).

If we observed different organizations and, in particular, VBOs, we would realize that the use of "signals" is an ordinary practice in their recruitment process. For example, it is quite common that someone who has worked as a volunteer is then hired by the organization. In fact, volunteer work can reduce the asymmetric information problem and reveal workers' intrinsic motivations. In the same way, the fact that a candidate for a job has previously participated in associative activities might have crucial importance in the recruitment process of a VBO, which is trying to select not only the ability of the workers but their vocation as well.

In these pages dedicated to VBOs, we examine with particular interest, the remedies suggested by economic theory for the part of *demand*. As regards recruitment, we are interested especially in the mechanisms that an organization can use to avoid the selection of "lemons" (as far as motivations and vocation are concerned).

One well-known theory spread in economic literature, refers to the wage policy. In the presence of information asymmetry, the employer might pay a wage *higher* than the expected value. In this way he hopes to recruit not only second-rate workers who are unable to guarantee the level of engagement needed. In fact, if we refer to our previous example, at a wage offer higher than $300 ($400, for example),[7] there is a certain probability that also "good" and not only "bad" candidates apply for the job.

However, this widespread and quite influential theory is based on an important assumption: that wage is the only factor which serves as an incentive for workers, the only "carrot" that attracts and motivates them. Such theory represents workers as individuals in only one dimension. There is no free space left in it for other forms of symbolic or ideal remuneration that are crucial, instead, within VBOs.

What happens, then, when we have to deal with organizations, such as VBOs, looking for men or women with a certain level of intrinsic motivations?

The VBO also often faces asymmetric information problems in its encounter with a new candidate for a certain job. For the reasons that we have already presented at the beginning of this work, it is interested in selecting those men who are prepared but who are *also* intrinsically motivated.

In the next paragraph, we will examine some possible solutions that economic theory offers in such cases.

"Get more by paying less"

In order to get more into the dynamics of the models (recently penetrating economic literature) that take into consideration not only instrumental motivations but non-monetary or immaterial behaviors as well, let us suppose that a company makes the hypothesis that a good candidate (one with "vocation") is not interested in wage and monetary incentives only (as standard theory assumes). A good candidate attributes, instead, added intrinsic value to the specific job he is applying for. Such intrinsic value is part of the satisfaction (or utility) he derives from the job. In other words, we can state that vocation is expressed in an *intrinsic reward* (not in a monetary or material one) that the individual gains from the performance of this specific activity.[8] Along this line of economics, workers' motivations are both intrinsic ("vocation") and instrumental (wage). Therefore, employees attribute different weights to them: a "good worker" would be the one who attributes positive value (>0) to the intrinsic component (while, according to standard theory, a worker who has no vocation is the one who values wage only).

The wage rate becomes not the only crucial factor for a candidate that the VBO intends to select when there are such motivations present.

According to Heyes, "vocation" is exactly that: "a desire by an individual to be directly engaged in the worthy activity" (Heyes 2005, p. 564). According to this author, two particular conditions must be met in order to define a worker who is intrinsically motivated:

1   Intrinsically motivated workers "go beyond the call of duty in doing their job" (ibid., p. 561);
2   Do this specific kind of job because they derive pleasure from it, and this "pleasure" is translated in the readiness to accept a lower wage (ibid.).

According to Heyes, for this same reason a "higher wage may attract the 'wrong sort' of person" (p. 568) Therefore, in the case of asymmetric information, by offering a lower wage, the company might stimulate the "good candidates" to self-select themselves.

At this point, let us make some initial conclusions concerning the selection of employees who have "vocation," according to this family of models:

•   If the wage rate offered by the VBO is lower than the market one, the fact that a person accepts it already indicates that her level of intrinsic motivation is greater than zero, since the difference in terms of well-being between the wage she could receive on the market and the lower one that she accepts instead working for the VBO, is compensated by the intrinsic satisfaction deriving from the job. The "remuneration gap" is filled up with the happiness of realizing one's "vocation." The fact that a person is ready to work without receiving any wage (as a volunteer, for example), is a sign that the entire well-being derived from this job can be explained with the intrinsic reward of her "vocation."[9]
•   If the VBO, instead, offers the market wage to candidates, remuneration in itself cannot guarantee that the organization is about to select the motivated individuals.
•   In such cases, however, the VBO could reward motivated workers (without exploiting their intrinsic motivations) as we do not have any reason to think that "good workers" would not accept a higher wage and that only "bad" ones would be finally selected.
•   Therefore, if the organization offers a wage lower than the market one, it can be certain that (at least in a context not characterized by structural unemployment)[10]: *it will not select any worker whose intrinsic motivation is equal to zero*. It is also aware that the more it reduces the wage rate, the more it would select workers whose intrinsic motivations are strong (if they accept this wage rate). And that if it was to offer a wage equal to zero, only workers with sole

intrinsic motivations would accept.[11] This conclusion is empirically proved by the wages earned by managers in the social economy sector.
- Finally, according to this branch of economic theory, if the organization was looking for people driven only by their intrinsic motivations, it would not have to pay any wages. It is gratuity that, in these cases, "selects" the best employees (as in the case of blood donation, when donated blood is of higher quality than that purchased on the market).[12]

These initial conclusions open some significant perspectives on the importance of volunteer work as well as on the reasons why organizations that focus on gratuity manage to attract particularly motivated and "good" workers. At such conclusions arrive the models that share the "getting more by paying less" slogan: the one of Katz and Handy (1998) concerning the selection of managers in the non-profit sector, or the Heyes' one (2005) concerning the wage policies in the English health-care sector (a model that enhances, in particular, the fact that the best nurses are the ones paid less).

The main assumption of these theoretic models is that *genuine motivations are directly proportional to one's readiness to sacrifice his material benefits* (wage). However, we can ask ourselves if the act of accepting a low wage is the right way of testing the intrinsic motivations or the "vocation" of a person? We will come back to this point at the end of this chapter. At this point, we mention only some criticisms of such theories made by some female economists (Nelson 2005, Folbre-Nelson 2000, Folbre-Weisskopf 1998). These scholars state that for a long time, the equivalence between genuineness and sacrifice has served as a cover for dominance and exploitation in the family as well as in traditional communities. According to them, such equivalence has been recently emerging once again—on the basis of some theoretic arguments—justifying lower wages in the health-care sector in which female workers are still predominant. According to this feminist critique, lower wages in the non-profit sector would allow only those women who are economically independent to cultivate their vocation, while other women with greater economic needs would be forced to accept other non-vocational jobs. Therefore, only wealthy women would have the possibility to cultivate their vocation. According to this critique, it is a mistake to think that an activity can be performed either "for love" or "for money," but not for both at the same time.[13]

Such considerations reveal some important limits of the "paying less" theories and stimulate us to find theoretic solutions more complex than the ones proposed by this group of models. This is what we will try to do in the next paragraphs.

When intrinsic motivations come into conflict with monetary incentives

We can render this model more sophisticated by taking into consideration the "motivational crowding-out effect."

The models presented until now are based on one assumption which is very common in economics but, at the same time, also very demanding from an anthropological point of view. It is that workers have two objectives: a material one (wage W) and a non-material one (intrinsic reward M) independent one from the other (can be added up).[14]

However, the empirical evidence shows that such a hypothesis is often unrealistic, mostly when we have to deal with values and activities based on "vocation." Such is the thesis of the Swiss economist Bruno Frey who gives some empirical evidence of the crowding-out effect of intrinsic motivations by monetary incentives in his book "Not just for money" (1997)—research entirely dedicated to this kind of situation. In the crowding-out theory, bad money (in this case, material incentives) drive out (or crowd out) good (intrinsic motivations).

By using some data, Frey shows us that a monetary reward could sometimes reduce, instead of increase, the commitment to a certain activity, in particular when its "vocational" aspects are crucial, thus when intrinsic motivations exist and are important. Psychologists give some different explanations of the crowding-out effect.

According to Deci and Ryan (1985, 2002), monetary rewards influence the self-determination and self-esteem of intrinsically motivated individuals, since in the presence of wages and material rewards they attribute to money their motivation for working. The underlying intuition is simple. Men do not always know how to attribute monetary value to their activities. If we asked, for example, a mother or a missionary what was the monetary value of assisting her child or listening to a poor man, their answer would probably be "I do not have any idea." The same would be the answer from our daughter if we asked her what was the monetary value of clearing the table.

However, if at a certain point parents start paying their daughter 5 euros for this activity, it is possible and probable, that she begins to attribute to it a value equal to 5 euros. If we decided to do the same thing in the case of a mother or a missionary, and remunerate their activity with a certain amount of money, we can be sure that they would both consider it to be a devaluation or dumping of their commitment (even if such amount is considerable). A similar phenomenon, although in different measure, occurs every time when we start remunerating volunteer workers, or when we support with incentives the environmental education, as well as in all those spheres in which civic virtues are at stake.[15]

Many experiments have been carried out in psychological studies proving the harmful effect of monetary rewards.[16]

In economics, Livernois and McKenna (1999) have showed that a higher compliance with pollution limits can be obtained by using lower fines in case of violations. Some recent economic experiments try to analyze situations of the principle-agent type. For example, Fehr and Gächter (2002) or Irlenbusch and Sliwka (2003) demonstrate that the principle's condition worsens and efficiency declines, if compared to the case of fixed wages, whenever incentives (such as bonuses and fines) are introduced.

We find some interesting hints in a study carried out by the economist Gneezy (2003). He built up an experiment by using a "proposer-respondent" game[17] with five different treatments. The proposer has to decide how much of the $24 to transfer to the other player. In the first treatment, called Dictator, the second player cannot either punish or offer a reward to the first player who makes the offer. He is obliged to accept the offer. In the "low fine" treatment if the second player is not satisfied with the offer, he can reduce up to 1.5 cents the gain of the first player (at a cost of 1 cent), while in the "high fine" treatment he can reduce (at the same cost) the proposer's gain up to 5 cents. If, for example, the first player offers $10 of his $24 to the second one, the latter can refuse a part of his own gain in order to reduce (or increase) the amount of $14 left to the former. The treatments in which rewards are possible are speculative. What were the results of Gneezy's experiment? On average, first player offers are bigger in the "dictator" treatment than in the "low fine" or "low reward" ones, and are biggest in the "high reward" or "high fine" treatments. As we can see in the graph below that shows the results from the experiment, called *The W Effect of Incentives* because of its trend, we can conclude that a small incentive has a negative effect on performance, while a bigger one has a positive effect. We can see in Figure 4.1 that the low average offers of the first player, the proposer, are associated with the "low fine" and "low reward" treatments.

Moreover, in one econometric study of volunteer work, Frey and Gotte (1999) show that monetary rewards cause its reduction.

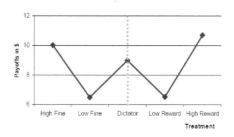

Figure 4.1 The W Effect of Incentives

Gneezy and Rustichini (2000a, 2000b) have performed some other interesting experiments in this field. The most famous one was conducted in 1998, lasted four months and involved 10 kindergartens in Haifa, Israel. As in all kindergartens around the world, also in these ones parents sometimes used to arrive late to pick up their children, after the closing time. Such delays were a burden for the teachers who had to stay in the kindergarten even after the end of their working hours. At a certain point, on advice of some economists and on the basis of the economic theory according to which fines can be used as an instrument to increase "price elasticity," in the kindergarten a fine was introduced in order to reduce delays. Contrary to the results expected, the introduction of the fine brought about a rise in delays by 40 percent. Why? The introduction of the fine changed the "frame" of the problem, that which was collective became completely personal, and allowed in this way the parents to "buy" the right to be late. However, the experiment did not finish like this: given the bad results, contrary to teachers' expectations, at a certain point (17 weeks after the beginning of the experiment) the fine was removed but the average delay did not diminish, did not "go back" and remained at the same levels as during the weeks in which the fine had been practiced: once a good becomes a commodity, it remains as such forever; there is a *hysteresis* on the way back to the initial position.

The second experiment concerns donations. In Israel, at a fixed date every year students arrange fundraising for social goals. In the experiment, the 180 students that had been preparing to participate in the fundraising, were divided into three groups. The students in the first group was simply told something about the importance of the task they were entrusted with.

In addition to this speech, the second group were promised 1 percent of the total funds collected at the end of the fundraising, while 10 percent was promised to the third group. Here are the results:

1st group: 238.6 (average amount collected by each student);
2nd group: 153.6;
3rd group: 219.33.

The students in the third group (who had been promised 10 percent of the total amount) gained more than the students in the second group (who had been promised 1 percent of the total amount) but less than the students in the first group. This empirical evidence shows us one more time that in some cases material incentives can have harmful effects on performance.

On the basis of the crowding-out theory, Frey explains these and other similar data that show that a wage increase might have either positive or negative effects on performance (the net effect will be positive whenever the wage increase incentive compensates the crowding-out effect on intrinsic motivations), while it seems that transition from free labor to some kind of monetary reward has a systematically negative impact on a worker's commitment. As the experiment conducted in an Israeli kindergarten proves, one of the consequences of such theory is the difficulty or even impossibility to "go back" to gratuity without reducing worker's well-being, once we have begun to remunerate a volunteer.

As regards the process of recruitment, what this model suggests is similar to what the models presented in the previous paragraph recommended: pay less or don't pay at all, at least in the beginning. In this case, however, the decision to pay less is not explained with the idea that intrinsic motivations fill up the differential between wage and "vocation." It is enhanced by the fact that when there are intrinsic motivations involved, it is possible that a high reward crowds them out.

But not even these relevant and striking findings of the motivation crowding theory can satisfy us totally (although they throw light on some important phenomena). Why? To give an example, let us think of a young volunteer worker who is forced after his marriage to seek paid employment. Aware of his intrinsic motivations, the organization in which he is a volunteer can easily offer to hire him so that it does not lose a worker who has "vocation." In this case, it seems implausible that motivational crowding-out effects occur. Generally speaking, a good theory should not put into an endemic conflict intrinsic and monetary motivations as if civil life was a "zero sum game" between economics and real sociality: this is exactly the content of the next section.

But what exactly is a worker's "vocation"?

In the end of our analysis of the recruitment mechanisms of individuals for whom work is "vocation" (the modern "Socrates"), the models examined leave open one crucial question: why should "vocation" be associated with the readiness to accept a lower wage? What is the theoretic justification for this assumption?

As a matter of fact, the cultural hypothesis underlying these models is related to one ancient and deep-rooted idea (that goes back at least to Smith[18]) according to which genuine sociality and intrinsic motivations do not fit in with the ordinary economic dynamics and market mechanisms. Therefore, if we want to introduce such intrinsic dimensions into the market, it is necessary to somehow "reduce" their economic component and leave in this way enough space for their authenticity. Motivation crowding theory is based on a similar assumption: instrumental motivations (to work because of the wage) and genuine ones (to work because of "vocation") are in conflict and tend to drive out or "crowd out" each other.

According to us, this interpretation embodies one "cultural vice": the fact that it considers economic and genuine dimensions of human actions in a structural conflict with each other. We do not think that such conflicting ideas of vocation and economic remuneration sends a good message to both economy and society, and in particular to people operating from a Civil Economy perspective according to which market represents just a stage of what we can call "civil" (Bruni and Zamagni 2007).

In this respect, we find an interesting and somehow different proposal in the model of the Australian economist Brennan (1996). Not to pay less, but to form instead the wage in a way that makes it more desirable to men for whom a job is a question of "vocation." In the case of academics (who are the subject of the study), Brennan observes that one way of inducing candidates to "self-select" themselves is to make a wage offer lower than the market one, but at the same time to fill the gap with some kind of fringe benefits (for example, research funds) which are selectively appreciated only by those who have a true academic "vocation."

Katz and Handy (in addition to the "paying less" instrument) suggest also this self-selecting mechanism (Katz and Handy 1998, p. 258), in particular in the academic field where "research-oriented professors will value research funding more than professors without such interest" (ibid.).

Likewise, Brennan divides the potential candidates into two categories: *true* scholars (S) "who attribute high value to the scientific success" (Brennan, p. 265) and the "Expedients" (E) "who are motivated only by the income deriving from academic work" (ibid.).

This line of research seems quite interesting from our perspective, since it does not state that vocation and market are necessarily conflicting or inconsistent with each other: Socrates is not paid less but differently, by using some more complex and sophisticated instruments to induce good candidates to self-selection.[19]

We will give more attention to these ideas, key elements of our work, later on. Anyway, to "pay differently" is a good way to go, even though in the case of VBOs the crucial question is rather: *which are* the forms of remuneration that stimulate the right ones among the candidates for a certain job to "self-select" themselves? In the case of academics, research funds could be one good instrument, but what kind of *fringe benefits* could be used in the case of a social cooperative, an NGO, an EoC company, etc?

What we suggest here is that we should go beyond the idea that *fringe benefits* are necessarily material (as in the case of research funds) and try to identify some other symbolic and relationship-based types of remuneration, which do not compensate for the lower wages but are rather a self-selection instrument in addition to wages.[20]

As a matter of fact, it is important to notice that not only VBOs look for people with "vocations" (Socrates) in the case of asymmetric information problems; *workers for whom job is vocation* (the Socrates) *are also looking for the right organization.* Therefore, symbolic signals have a dual nature: they allow both the "announcement" of the company's ideal mission and the self-selection of the candidates.

In this sense, the organizational culture and governance seem to play a key role in VBOs. The well-rendered, high and accountable ideal *mission*, could be an important signal that attracts people with "vocation." Isn't it true—and the evidence is there for all—that when an organization or a community are an expression of high ideals, they attract "men of quality," and when such ideals are in crisis, they attract "strange" ones instead? And that it is somehow already too late for them whenever they start to attract the wrong ones? As a matter of fact, we should honestly make the conclusion that, whenever an organization stops attracting "Socrates," its ideal crisis is already at an advanced stage. The difficulty in attracting people who have "vocation" is already a symptom (and not the reason) of the fact that the organization's ideals are at crisis point, or that they are at least not observable from the outside anymore.

We can summarize that *mission* represents the general culture of an organization which becomes the real signal capable of inducing new candidates to "self-select" themselves; the appearance of candidates lacking in vocation is a sign that the organization's culture is not attractive anymore and, therefore, it is necessary to act on this identity and foundation level to pass from the vicious to the virtuous circle.

Obviously, this is not the most positive closing message of a chapter in which various ways of attracting men for whom work is a matter of "vocation" to VBOs have been examined; but it is surely a message that could be useful to prevent such phenomena from occurring.

Finally, let us pose one "uncomfortable" question, especially at this point of our work: can we be sure that "vocation" is something (a fact or characteristic trait) that is present in men *before* they start a certain kind of job, that it is somehow an initial endowment of the worker related to his nature and life story; or is it possible to imagine, instead, that "vocation" is one at least partially endogenous component of a certain job or activity)? As a matter of fact, it is possible to distinguish one's job preferences *ex-ante* (before starting it) and one's attitude towards this same job *ex-post* (after starting it). Let us once again think about the "market" of academics. Is it necessary to identify the "vocation" of a candidate (for example, the dedication to students as well as to research) during the recruitment process by offering a lower wage or we could suppose, instead, that, once they have been hired, the academics would recognize that it is their duty to commit themselves to research and dedicate a part of their time to students? Here we could also talk about nurses, firefighters, school teachers and many other professions.

VBOs, incentives, and rewards

In this section, we go deeper into the delicate relationship between motivations and incentives and we resume an ancient topic which we consider to be important in the case of VBOs: the "reward" that we will try to distinguish from "incentive."

But let us start with the question: what exactly is an incentive?

"Incentive" is actually an ancient word. During the Middle Ages *incentivus* (from *incinere*, sing and enchant) was a wind instrument, the flute in general, to which the voices of the choir had to be adjusted. The flute is also the tool of the snake-charmer whose snake gets bewitched by its sweet sound and goes obediently where the sound leads it. The use of the *incentivus* was then extended from the flute to the trumpet and for dictating the pace of running for soldiers in battle. The incentive, therefore, is something that spurs us on, makes us eager or urges us to bold action, something that enchants us with its sound and makes us go where the one who is playing the instrument wants to take us. The incentive presents itself as a free contract, and this is why it is fascinating. The capitalist company proposes a pay or career scheme, and we, workers "freely" accept it. The aim, as the ancient root suggests, is to harmonize the various members of the company, i.e. to make sure that the employee's behaviour aligns with the set goal of the owners, and in the absence of this agreement, the objectives and actions would naturally become divergent, discordant and forgotten.

Incentives are mainly monetary and are connected with performance: you receive one when you reach a certain level of performance or productivity. The initial assumption of the theory of incentives is that the interests of workers or members of an organization are rarely aligned with those of its managers and founders. One of the authors who has mostly dealt with this topic, Campbell,[21] makes an interesting example. He points out that the pilot of an aircraft is determined as much as the passengers to arrive safe and sound at the destination. In this case a spontaneous alignment of interests occurs. But the well-being of the mechanic on earth might be not directly correlated to the passengers' interests. Therefore, passengers need to be reassured that the mechanic intends to operate according to their security interests. From this example, Campbell draws the conclusion that without incentives, or with inappropriate ones, the mechanic could be tempted to avoid the most difficult or boring operations and, thus, inspect and repair the aircraft only superficially. Therefore, incentives and fines become crucial instruments of resolving similar problems in every single type of organization and not only when mechanics are concerned: they shall be the reason of the organization's vitality, no matter how big or small it is.

To understand the nature of the ideology of incentives it is necessary, however, to look at its history that does not originate from the tradition of economic sciences but emerged from among the scientific theories of management. These started to develop in the U.S. around the 20s, that is, between the two world wars and in the presence of fascism, totalitarianism and collectivism. A phase of civil and anthropological pessimism similar to the one Machiavelli and Hobbes lived in, generated a theory based on a pessimistic and thrifty way of thinking about human nature. The logic of incentives was first received with strong controversy and heated ethical debates, which however, soon fell silent. During the Cold War, the control of people by incentives appeared in fact as a vaccine against a disease that appeared to be much more serious. Control and planning within organizations were the small dose of poison ingested for protection from the possibly deadly virus of totalitarian planning and control by an illiberal system that was establishing itself in the other part of the world. So it was considered a necessary evil to make sacrifices of freedom and equality inside companies in order to keep up the capitalist system and democracy. Political democracy was defended by sacrificing economic democracy. Freedom in society, but central planning inside enterprises. Today collectivist systems are history, yet their vaccine continues to be injected into our bodies, and it works well beyond the scope of the largest industrial enterprises for which it was originally invented.

The main, large and harmful side effect of the ideology of incentives is that it created a realm of human relations in which there is nothing anymore that has an intrinsic value, something that shows as valuable before the cost-benefit calculation. There is a second crucial element called power. The alignment produced by incentives is not reciprocal. It is the powerful party that sets out the objectives and designs the incentive scheme, while the weaker party is only required to align with the magical singing of the charmer. Incentives are therefore offered by those in power to those who do not have the power to control their actions, motivations and freedom. It is the nature of incentives to provide unilateral power for the management and no reciprocity between equals; and its function is control, not freedom. Unions, for example, cannot understand a lot of the reasons for their current crisis and they will not be able to rediscover their vocation unless they interpret the world of work within the framework of this new ideology.

Finally, the culture of incentives reduces the anthropological and spiritual complexity of the person. The great classical culture knew that there are many human motivations and they cannot be traced back to a single meas-uring means, let alone money. It also knew that using money to motivate people inevitably tends to reduce intrinsic motivation after some time, and thus it greatly impoverishes organizations, society and people who have an infinite value because they know how to find more forms of value in things and in themselves. In fact, it would take many instruments to tune people well within organizations and to bring them into agreement with each other, including, of course, the flute of incentives, but only in harmony with the violin of respect, the oboe of *philia*, the viola of gratitude. Because if there is only one instrument to play, then biodiversity, creativity, generosity, and freedom will be lost in the workplaces, and you end up forcing your people to produce less beautiful sounds and boring, sad melodies.

The issue of incentives is quite controversial, especially in the case of VBOs. As a matter of fact, this theory is based on several assumptions, among which two seem to be crucial: (1) each worker tends to do as little as possible, since work is considered to be something bad, and increases his own well-being by avoiding it[22]; (2) motivations and incentives can be added up: incentives can be added to other kinds of motivations present in the person.

But there is something more—and less well known to say—about incentives.

Incentives, motivations, and VBOs

As we have seen in the previous paragraphs, when intrinsic motivations or ideals are present, incentives may sometimes have controversial and even harmful effects on motivations. The (ii) assumption of the incentive theory, thus, is not empirically confirmed. As a matter of fact, the introduc-tion of incentives in order to increase the single members' productivity in organizations that focus on cooperation based on "ideal" objectives, such as VBOs, may be counterproductive if it triggers competitive dynamics and crowds out the crucial for every VBO members' sense of the organiza-tion as a whole, the sense of "us." Such an assumption is rooted in a line of economic and psychological literature analyzing decision-making and *frame* process, whose leading exponents are March (1995), Messick (1999), Messick and Tenbrunsel (1996) and Cialdini (1996).

The basic idea of this theory is that men's reactions differ according to the specific *frame* in which a certain decision has to be made. The role of the *frame* in regards to human reasoning can be compared to the one of Cartesian axes in a graph: it confines our reasoning to the area of possibil-ity and logic. For example, collaboration with others certainly becomes an important element if the frame "us" is active in those who make decisions.

As regards social dilemmas and cooperation, the above-mentioned authors claim that the introduction of incentives or fines sets off the *individualistic frame* of competition and, consequently, makes cooperation decrease.[23]

Another type of empirical analysis can strengthen the hypothesis that material rewards might reduce the sense of "us." We refer to the survey of Italian non-profit organizations conducted by Borzaga and Depedri (2005), Borzaga and Tortia (2004). Among other facts, in the survey has been observed that job satisfaction (which is directly connected to workers' loyalty to the organization) is influenced by the job's relationship aspects that "produce a sense of belonging to the group, of involvement in the organization's *mission* and of integration" (Borzaga and Tortia 2004, p. 15). At the same time, we should note that there is a sort of *trade-off* between relationship-based incentives (that here we call intrinsic) and extrinsic ones: if incentives are continuously implemented, they tend to reduce the sense of belonging, the intrinsic motivation and the workers' feeling of the organization's mission as their own.

Given the specific nature of VBOs, it becomes, on one hand, necessary to keep their members highly motivated by recognizing and rewarding their commitment. On the other hand, however, it is necessary to pay particular attention to the instruments (such as rewards) that have been used, so that they do not have the opposite effects. When no attention is paid to the 2 percent which differentiate VBO from other types of organization, there is the risk to use instruments that can cause the loss of its identity or the decrease in its ideal quality.

Therefore, one crucial element is to find the right way to preserve motivations and to avoid that individual incentives transform the members' nature. That means to avoid that cooperative agents with a strong sense of "us" turn into "I" individuals interested only in their own remuneration (both material or fringe benefits). As a matter of fact, a paradox may occur: once the members of a VBO, the cooperative culture mostly depends on, have been identified, managers try to strengthen their motivations by using incentives and rewards. However, if they make a mistake with the kind of incentives used (individual and monetary, for example), they end up to transform the nature of these members' motivations. They start to think more and more in terms of "I" and of individual advantages. Although good, their initial intention to strengthen further the most motivated members by using incentives, transforms them over time into individuals who are less interested in the real good of the organization, in "us." That is why, incentives are really delicate and have to be used very carefully within VBOs. It is useless to simply try to imitate capitalistic companies in which, as a matter of fact, they always work less. The most important thing to take into account in developing strong networks that sustain the life and progress of VBOs is the relationship effects of incentives (both individual and collective ones).

We have already seen that the: (i) assumption is an important issue within VBOs. Intrinsic motivations are generally high and might be in conflict with incentives. Therefore, we should still verify the (ii) assumption (according to which labor is considered something bad and workers seek to do as little as possible). We now try to outline the meaning of this remaining assumption within VBOs in order to find out whether it is fundamental or not.

Once again, we start with a question: *what do we call "work"?*

First of all, "work" is a human activity. It is, therefore, impossible to say something in its regard without clarifying what we call "human" or a human being, without taking anthropology into account.

We are convinced that, in particular in VBOs, but in any other kind of activity as well, *we do really work when the recipient of the fruits of our work is "someone else."*

If work is a human activity and if we can call really "human" what is love and, thus, gives itself away to others, then *we do really work when our activity is an expression of love.* Therefore, "to work for" can be seen as the necessary condition (even though not sufficient, as we will see further on) to talk about work in the perspective presented here. That is why we do not call children's games or our hobby "work." But we do describe like this housewives' or volunteers' activity. And we do not think of an activity, based on intrinsic motivations only, as "work" until someone else considers it valuable and is even ready to pay or do something for it.

Moreover, we see that there are many different dimensions of this "to work for." First of all, it means not only to work for "you" who I find in front of me, who I see and with whom I have a personal relationship. It means also to work for "him" or for "her" who I will probably never see or who I will not be able to recognize even if I meet them. It means to work also for the patient who will need the laboratory of my clinic, for the client who will use my product or for an unborn child.

We start to work *really* when we work for *someone else.* And we believe that it is exactly in this fact that the true dignity of human work consists. We work *really* when we forget about our personal interests and we give ourselves away to others.

And if we see work and rewards from this perspective, then we can go beyond the issue of alignment of the interests. If I work for "you" and for "him" or "her," then I do not work for myself only and I do my job with dignity. Therefore, "my" interests become a part of "our" interests in a context of fraternity and mutual advantage.

All of this does not mean that we are naïve and ignore the presence of opportunistic traits in all human beings, even in the most motivated ones. It rather means that we should recognize that work is not only something *bad.* It mostly is an expression of our activities and our life, especially when we share the ideals of the organization we work for. But even in such contexts some conflicts may occur; we will analyze them extensively in the second part of this book.

Incentives or awards (*premi*)?

If the arguments presented up to now were valid (especially those concerning recruitment), we could say that potential members and workers of a VBO are the ones who see "work" as an expression of vocation, who are animated by passion and intrinsic motivations. A first possible conclusion could be that in VBOs there is no need to use incentives in order to control and align the different interests present. On the contrary, the use of incentives would produce results opposite to the ones desired.

At the same time, there is some empiric evidence that shows how in VBOs a flat-rate remuneration, equal for everyone, could be just as demotivating. What shall we do?

By conducting various experiments, it has been proved that in the presence of strong intrinsic motivations, monetary rewards might cause the deterioration in someone's performance when perceived as an instrument of control. If reward is perceived as a "prize" and recognition, instead, it nourishes motivations and performance. Intrinsic motivations tend to decrease especially when retribution is linked to the performance of a specific task or to the achievement of a certain goal. In such cases it is as if the person was concentrated only on the results ("how much" and "how") of a certain activity and not on "why" he performs it. Moreover, the value of reward, especially if it is a monetary one, is perceived as the value of what one is doing and of how much does it cost, and all this discourages his commitment. That is why the paid collection of blood for transfusions is generally less efficient than voluntary donations (Titmuss 1970).

We need to ask the following question: is there some way of preserving VBOs members' high motivations without incurring the crowding-out effect? The answer that we try to give is that if remuneration was perceived by those who receive them, as a sign of recognition and appreciation and, thus, as a "reward," it would have positive effects on commitment. But what is the difference between *rewards* and *incentives*?

One hard challenge for the managers of VBOs who want to keep their members highly motivated, is to know in which way to reward without making them feel somehow controlled. The reward is a recognition, it is like saying—in different languages and with creativity—*Thank you: you are important and precious for this organization and for all of us*.

But one question still remains open (and will remain open even after the conclusion of this book): how can we distinguish incentives from rewards?

In this regard, we can refer to one eminent author of the *Civil Economy* tradition: Giacinto Dragonetti.

In 1766, shortly after the publication of Cesare Beccaria's book *On crimes and punishments*, Giacinto Dragonetti, a young lawyer from Aquila, Italy, published in Naples a book entitled *On virtues and rewards*.

Contemporary economic theory of action is based on individual *incentives*. Dragonetti advanced a theory of action based on *awards*. Such a theory proceeds from the hypothesis that good (or virtuous) citizens act also for intrinsic reasons. Unlike modern incentives, "awards," in fact, are not the ex-ante "motivation" for a given action but an ex-post recognition or prize. Contemporary economics registers a new tiny interest in the issue of awards or rewards, a reason more for a re-evaluation of Dragonetti's forgotten book. The work of Bruno Frey, in particular, is bringing the issue of awards back to the attention of economists (Frey and Neckermann 2008; Neckermann et al. 2009), although the economics community has not yet recognized this branch of research.

Giacinto Dragonetti (1738–1818), a lawyer and disciple of Antonio Genovesi, was born in L'Aquila. Under Genovesi's supervision the young Dragonetti published *A Treatise on Virtues and Award*s ("Delle virtù e de' Premi"), in Naples in 1766, shortly after Beccaria's *On Crimes and Punishments* ("Dei delitti e delle pene," 1764). By 1769 an edition of Dragonetti's book with the original Italian text and an English translation was already circulating.[24] In 1776, in his influential *Common Sense,* Thomas Paine cited the book, referring to Dragonetti as "that wise observer on governments" (1923[1776], p. 30). But, after his early fame, Dragonetti was almost forgotten even in his homeland, and the issues concerning the relationship between awards and virtues were likewise neglected (Bruni 2013).

The introduction of Dragonetti's book provides a clear point of entry to his vision of virtues and awards: "We have made numberless laws to punish crimes, and not one is established to reward virtue" (1769, p. 13).[25]

Although the title of the book (*On Virtues and Rewards*) may be interpreted as an attempt to counter Beccaria's argument (*On Crimes and Punishments*), an accurate reading of the two books reveals the same specific intention—to address an aspect that had been overlooked. Furthermore, Beccaria was not totally oblivious to the positive implications of rewarding virtue, but he does confine this topic to the margins of his inquiry. The theme of rewards arises towards the end of *On Crimes and Punishments*, in a section about crime prevention:

> Another means of preventing crimes is to reward virtue. I notice that the laws of all nations today are totally silent on this matter. If the prizes awarded by academies to the discoverers of useful truths have

increased both knowledge and the number of good books, why should not prizes distributed by the beneficent hand of the sovereign likewise increase the number of virtuous actions? In the hands of the wise distributor, the coin of honor will prove a lasting investment.

(Beccaria 1995[1764], p. 109)

Beccaria's analysis of "prizes" contains yet another remark about the importance of education: "Finally, the surest but hardest way to prevent crime is to improve education" (ibid.), an instrument closely linked to the reward of virtue, an issue dear to most Enlightenment thinkers (especially Genovesi). Beccaria and others only mentioned the reward of virtue without exploring it further,[26] whereas Dragonetti, inspired by a more radical and far-reaching approach, devoted his analysis entirely to this disregarded issue. Dragonetti envisioned an entire system of laws built around the idea of rewarding virtue ("political virtue" in particular): *a code of virtue* to go alongside the penal code. "The Roman law-givers knew the necessity of recompenses, but contented themselves with hinting at them, without courage to form their code"[27] (1769, p. 13).

It is also clear that Dragonetti's point was not to deny the importance of punishment; like Genovesi, he recognized its crucial role. But Dragonetti was convinced that concentrating on punishment principally or exclusively would not be enough to get the Kingdom of Naples back on a path of civil and economic growth.

More generally, the different positions of Beccaria and Dragonetti can also be explained in terms of their respective philosophical traditions. In fact, while Beccaria's framework is essentially consistent with the first elements of the utilitarian doctrine, Dragonetti has to be interpreted within the classical tradition of the virtue ethics (in line with Aristotle, Cicero, and Thomas Aquinas). And if Beccaria echoes Hobbes in his characterization of the state of nature:

Laws are the terms under which independent and isolated men come together in society. Wearied by living in an unending state of war and by a freedom rendered useless by their uncertainty of retaining it, they sacrifice a part of that freedom in order to enjoy what remains in security and calm.

(Beccaria 1995[1764], p. 9)

The vision of sociality and the essence of the social contract that emerge in Dragonetti follow the works of Genovesi and the Thomistic-Aristotelian view of civil virtues as natural to humankind. Dragonetti hoped to revive interest in the reward of civil virtue that had characterized the Roman republicanism of Cicero and Plutarch and that emerges also in certain expressions of the Lockean tradition.[28]

In this classical tradition, a virtue (*areté*) is a disposition or character trait of an individual, defined generally relative to a particular domain, according to the *telos* or, in today's words, the intrinsic nature of that domain. Furthermore, the logic behind the classical view of virtue diverges from both the instrumentalist and the consequentialist accounts. A virtuous person pursues *areté* for an intrinsic reason, and not for the sake of pleasure or other material rewards. At the same time, a virtuous action may also indeed yield pleasure and material rewards, but they are an indirect result, a sort of by-product of the virtuous conduct (Bruni and Sugden 2011).

Therefore, there is nothing in the classical theory of virtue that impedes also considering *virtues* (dispositions or character traits that help to promote excellence-*areté* and approval in the economic domain), as Dragonetti does (and as most of the communitarian literature today does not: Bruni and Sugden 2013). Unlike most contemporary accounts of civil virtue, which seem to favor an intrinsic notion of rewards,[29] for Dragonetti the reward of virtue has a civil and "public" nature, and is somehow external to the virtuous agent: "Nor ought it to be objected, that virtue, in proposing its price, loses its dignity and becomes mercenary" (ibid.).

In other words, it is possible to reward civil virtues without the risk of reducing the gratuitousness of virtuous acts to a mere counter-service of a ("mercenary") exchange, which would otherwise compromise the spontaneous, genuine, non-mandatory, essentially free character of virtue—this issue has arisen frequently (and controversially) in the lively debate over the proper reward of "vocational" activities.

So what is the thing that Dragonetti wanted to enhance when he was postulating the importance of recognizing the reward of virtues? The main difference between the modern economics term "incentives" and Dragonetti's *premi* is the contrast between individual and social. Incentives are individuals-based, designed around private self-interest (only as an indirect or unintentional effect might they also yield benefits of some sort for the common good). The nature of an incentive scheme is purely extrinsic, by nature a private principal-agent relation. *Premi*-awards, instead, are public or civil by nature; they are given when someone has performed intentionally an action for some form of common good. They must be assigned publicly, in presence of an audience, and the value of an award is directly proportional to its publicity and social approval. This social approbation and recognition is the greater part of the value assigned to an award.

There is another crucial element in Dragonetti's notion of *premi*. In harmony with the Civil Economy tradition, he claimed that actions whose aim is the public good are not in contrast, at least in principle, with self-interest (despite these being two separate objectives, and not necessarily interrelated); nor is public good in any way incompatible with individual interest or incentives. *Awards go hand in hand with rewards*. In considering the Roman republic or the Greek *polis*, Dragonetti notices that "Public grandeur was not concentrated in a few, but expanded itself with such power, that each private interest was dissolved in the public, and each ray of the public reflected on its members" (ibid., p. 29).

Hence his own definition of rewards: "Rewards alone tie the wayward interest of individuals to the public, and keep the eye of man intent on general good" (ibid., p. 31).

Therefore, despite acknowledging the distinction between acts motivated by virtue and those motivated by self-interest, Dragonetti never saw these two kinds of actions as opposed or in any way incompatible. It is fair to say that, in his view, a good society ought to be able to reconcile self-interest and virtue, rewards and awards, contracts and gratuitousness.

Nowadays, we can find some traces of Dragonetti's idea to award virtues in the branch of law known as *premial law*. It concerns the special merits which society ascribes to some men praised for their exemplary and virtuous behavior or life-style, and rewards in different ways and through different institutions—honorifics, civic or military medals, academic and scholastic awards, commutation of sentences for civilly virtuous behaviors, and many more—that are abundant in traditional (and monarchic) societies, and elements that complicate the possibility of reconsideration of that old idea of *premi*.

A key point that makes Dragonetti's ideas relevant in the contemporary ethical debate concerning markets is the connection he makes between markets and civil virtue. As he uses the term, *premi* conveys a meaning associated with both *award* and *reward*, although in an unusual and original way.

Both Genovesi and Dragonetti, and the tradition of Civil Economy as a whole, regarded commerce as a key opportunity for cultivating and *rewarding* civil virtue. If market is construed in the Civil Economy tradition as a form of "mutual assistance," then commerce itself becomes a virtue because by trading and contributing to developing the market, individuals are ultimately contributing to the common good. Moreover, starting a commercial activity in eighteenth-century Naples required the ability to take risks, and this gesture too may be interpreted as a token of public virtue since the entire community benefits from its results. From the perspective of Civil Economy, the market is a place where virtues can be encountered and cultivated. Market and trade are both essential to public happiness. As Dragonetti notes, "Commerce is the reciprocal communication of the produce and industry of various countries ... The citizens of earth carry on a war of industry against each other, and where that ceases, there the supports of life decay" (1769, pp. 113, 121).

For this reason, society ought to recognize commercial virtues and publicly reward virtuous merchants, as in ancient Rome where the best merchants were allowed to join the equestrian order.

> Commerce influences the manners. Its spirit is that of frugality, moderation, prudence, tranquility, order. Whilst these subsist riches are harmless. Commerce has every where propagated the study of social habits ... If these are the advantages of the commerce, *the trader should not want his reward*.[30]

> (p. 131, our italics)

Neglecting to reward commercial virtues would discourage market transactions and, therefore, diminish the market as an institution; and without markets there can be no public happiness. Dragonetti treats the subjects of war and navigation in similar terms (1769, p. 78 ff.). Without adequate defence and naval trade there can be no safe commerce; therefore defence should not be left to mercenary troops, rewarding instead the pure military virtues which keep the state safe and, hence, free and happy. A similar attitude emerges at the conclusion of an unpublished letter written by Dragonetti to his brother Gian Battista, who had asked him about the link between the first and the second part of his book: "If I did not discuss agriculture, war, navigation and commerce, that are the ... main human virtues, what would my ... little treatise be worth?" (Dragonetti, quoted in Italian in Bruni [2010]).[31]

The implication of this vision of commerce, which was quite common in Europe at that time (as Hirschman (1977) and others have explained[32]), is that Dragonetti regards commerce as part of the system for the reward of virtue.[33] It is virtuous to satisfy other people's needs, and by facilitating mutually advantageous transactions the market rewards virtue.

His chapter on commerce, recalling a very old and popular thesis on commerce that, thanks to a providential design, springs from the differences among nations, states:

> A thousand proofs convince us that man was made for society, but above all, the mutual dependence on mutual wants, that basis of all unions ...

> The barrenness of one place is to be supplied by the fertility of another, and industrious nations provide for the want of slothful ones. Without commerce trade is impossible. Commerce is the reciprocal communication of the produce and industry of various countries ...

> To make each individual participate of the benefits of the nature, and to give to the political body all the strength is capable of, ought to be the effect of the commerce.

> (pp. 113, 122, 123)

One possible and legitimate reading of such passages on commerce, in line again with the fundamental concept of the Civil Economy tradition, is that the market is a key mechanism for rewarding virtues.

From that perspective, market and trade are perfectly moral or virtuous, and mutual advantage, reciprocity, and morality go hand- in-hand. From this perspective, although the Civil Economy tradition emphasizes virtue and its reward, it follows a different cultural path than the one held by "communitarian" authors such as E. Anderson, M. Walzer (1983), M. Sandel or A. McIntyre (1981). These authors, instead, see a contrast between true moral relationship and standard economic or market interactions. For Dragonetti (and Genovesi), however, market and virtues are fully consistent one another (Bruni and Sugden 2013).

Finally, how could we imagine the rewards of virtues as a road to economic and civil development? As a road to the blossom of VBOs?

A first possibility is to remunerate correctly civic virtues, to promote cooperative behaviors and discourage non-cooperative and opportunistic ones. Unlike incentives which evaluate the merit and enhance the competitiveness among workers, rewards, as we have defined them, are a *recognition* for virtuous behaviors and engagement with cooperation. Incentives are based on an evaluation system of the individual performance. Rewards, instead, exceed incentives as they recognize the efforts of a certain group to collaborate and achieve the organization's goals. If we think of a school, to establish a system of incentives could mean to predetermine certain objectives (concerning education quality in regard to teachers and productivity in regard to the support staff) and to adequately remunerate those who manage to achieve such objectives.

Along the line reopened nowadays by Bruno Frey, we can say that rewards are a way of recognizing the "exceeding" component which characterizes civilly virtuous actions. They can consist of titles, medals, recognition, etc., that increase the well-being and happiness of those who receive them. As Dragonetti explicitly states, their main goal is to foster such civic actions in a certain group or community in relation to the anti-civic ones. Reward is usually a communitarian form of remuneration (and not a purely individual one) which strengthens the sense of loyalty and belonging to the school (in the case we refer to). It could consist of a travel prize, as a possibility to improve one's studies, in flexible timetables that help to reconcile work and family, or in more attention paid to voluntary activities of the workers, etc.

However, sometimes a simple "Thank you" told to the person who collaborates in a VBO at the expense of many often hidden sacrifices, told in the presence of others (acknowledgement that does not remain confined to the private relationship is important) can be a support of the internalization of civic virtues. At the same time, "Thank you" cannot be the only or the main reward given by the organization to workers and even volunteers. VBOs' managers need to be creative in order to invent rewards richer and more complex than a "Thank you," rewards that do not discourage motivations, but strengthen them instead.

We would like to close this chapter with this open question. It is true that, from one point of view, the life stories, cultures and identities of men are different and the word "vocation" expresses exactly this diversity: not all of us would either spend 40 years taking care of the ill, or dedicate their life to the research of new galaxies; and not all of us would give our life to the poor trying to build up a better world. At the same time, it is also true that there are many other aspects which go beyond these diversities and gather human beings together making it possible that a person, in particular a young person, flourishes and finds out his own vocation while working in "alive" and "positive" organizations. And that, on the contrary, fades away becoming indifferent and opportunistic over time, if the organization's culture is cynical and sad.

There is no VBO without Socrates; but once it exists, it is the VBO itself, with its particular dynamics and culture, that knows how to create Socrates by bringing out each person's own "*daimon*." In order to achieve this high goal, incentives cannot be enough.

Notes

1 We do not discuss here this dimension of recruitment also because it is the main subject of thousands of works in economics. We make the assumption that the VBO has already solved the problem of selecting capable candidates. The selection of people who have "vocation" concerns those individuals who have already passed the test of professional adequacy (Katz and Handy 1998 for example), assumes that the organization tests first the theoretic preparedness and capacity of the candidates and only the ones who pass this test enter the second stage of the process of recruitment, the "vocational" one.

2 In this study, we do not distinguish managers from employees in order to avoid also treating the complex problem of conflict of interests that might occur between "principal" and "agent." A VBO can be a cooperative or an association of small dimensions in which, independently of their specific tasks that may change over time, all employees share the same level of participation.

3 This law used to become operative in the presence of "shorn coins" (gold or silver coins filed in order to remove a little bit of metal) or when in a moment of institutional change there were more than one legal coin circulating within the State (for example, the brief co-existence of euro and lira).

4 Therefore, the process of driving good money out of the market was due to the fact that within it both good and bad money had the same price. Given the common awareness of the probability to encounter bad money during the market exchange and the impossibility to recognize it, the price of money set on the market is lower than the one practiced in the case only good money were present. Moreover, this price is higher than the one set in case only bad money

were present on the market. That is why who owned good money did not accept the exchange because it seemed iniquitous to him. At the same time—and here is the point—those who owned bad money were strongly encouraged to use them—(since the price offered was higher than the "right" one corresponding to the real value of their money). Akerlof (1970, p. 490) adds that the analogy between the asymmetric information and Gresham's law is only partial, as the difference between good and bad money is, in fact, observable (for example, in their different weight, or in the more complex case of euro-lira). As a matter of fact, the monetary phenomenon observed by the English financier Thomas Gresham (1519–1579) and before him by the eminent Polish astronomer Nicolò Copernico in 1525, as well as, almost 2000 years earlier, by the Greek playwright Aristophanes (in *The Frogs*), concerned phenomena different from the ones in which Akerlof was interested, even though the information problem that stands on their bases is the same.

5 This mechanism can explain, for example, why the price of an used car decreases considerably if only a few days after its purchase, the buyer decides to put it up for sale. In this case a loss of market value occurs. It is much bigger than the simple physical deterioration or obsolescence of the car.

6 We use the expression "labor market" by convention. However, it is sometimes useful to be reminded, also in the economic literature, that labor is more than a commodity exchanged on the market.

7 We make the hypothesis here that the reservation wages (the minimum wage rate at which a worker would be willing to accept the job) are distributed along a continuum.

8 Using a slightly more formal language, we can say that the preferences of a "good candidate" (in this case the one who is intrinsically motivated) can be represented by the following utility function: $L=\alpha W + (1-\alpha)M$, where W stands for wage; M stands for the individual's intrinsic reward deriving from the performance of the VBO's specific activity; α stands for the weight attributed to wage; and $1-\alpha$ stands for the weight of the intrinsic motivation of the worker (which, according to our hypothesis, is negatively correlated to the weight attributed to wage).

9 In this case, the value of the α parameter from the equation presented in the previous note would be equal to 1.

10 When there is unemployment on the labor market, things get more complicated as there is no guarantee that candidates without "vocation" have a better alternative (in terms of wage rate). Therefore, it is possible that the company attracts "standard" workers, who although lacking in "vocation," are ready to accept a lower wage rate than the reservation wage just because they are unemployed. In such a context (let us think, for example, of the market of labor in some Italian regions), the low wage policy cannot be used as an instrument of selection of the motivated workers.

11 This conclusion is not particularly different from the one made in standard economic theory (the so called "efficiency wage"). In this case, however, the company has to pay less (and not more) than the amount paid on the market, in order to attract the best workers.

12 It is thus desirable that the organization sees the volunteer as a genus that is different from the paid worker. His remuneration, professional qualification and responsibilities are, therefore, also different. If the two markets overlap instead, the crowding-out effect might easily occur. From this point of view, gratuity does not correspond to a zero price, but to an infinite one instead.

13 In other works (Bruni and Sugden 2008), some distinctions between the Nelson, communitarianist and Civil Economy's approach, have been presented.
14 It is possible, therefore, to present them as a summation.
15 We can notice that in these fields of human action, money can strengthen intrinsic motivation only if it is perceived as a gift (and not as a price). Frey calls this effect "crowding-in."
16 Cf. Deci and Ryan 1985; Lepper and Greene 1978; Sansone and Harackiewicz 2000.
17 In this kind of game, an initial amount is available to the A player (proposer). A can decide if and how much of this amount to transfer to B (respondent). B himself can decide to accept or reject the offer of A. If B rejects, both A and B gain nothing.
18 Cf. Bruni and Sugden (2008).
19 Along this line of research, we find also the names of authors like Hargreaves-Heap (2000).
20 If there were no real budget constraint in the world of social economy we would have no theoretic reason not to apply the same labor standards as those in the private and public sector to the employees of the values-based companies. Low wages are a matter of real-life and not just theory. The danger that underlies the paying less models is to give a theoretical justification of a situation which is in reality unfair, due to a lack of funds and resources.
21 Cf. Campbell (1995).
22 Lane (1991), p. 349 claims that people would never work without rewards.
23 Messick and Tenbrunsel (1999) prove this hypothesis in some experiments.
24 Dragonetti's book is undoubtedly the result of a dialogue with Genovesi and the Neapolitan Economia Civile school and *On Virtues and Rewards* may well have been written under Genovesi's supervision. This was the opinion of Alfonso Dragonetti, who in a short biography of his great-uncle Giacinto writes: "In 1760 he came to Naples to receive an education that would prepare him for a career in the practice of law and he engaged in the study of jurisprudence in the spirit of philosophical inquiry … The illustrious Genovesi was then a master of reasoning, not just in Naples, but in Italy, and it was under his guidance that the young mind from l'Aquila was educated to mature reflection and exact thinking" (Dragonetti 1847, p. 113).
25 The quotations from Dragonetti's Delle virtù e de' Premi come from the English 1769 edition. Genovesi's translations in this book, awaiting the forthcoming English translation of his Lezioni, are ours.
26 For example, Montaigne, Hobbes, Rousseau, Montesquieu, and later Diderot, Bentham, Filangieri, Gioja, and others; or, in ancient times, the Roman philosophers and legal experts who Dragonetti also recalled. The issue is central in the Civil Economy tradition in the Kingdom of Naples.
27 In a note Dragonetti recalls the famous phrase from the Digest, Lib. I.l.I § I. Tit. I: "Endeavouring to make men good, not by the fear of punishment only, but likewise by the incentives of reward" (ibid.).
28 Echoes of this tradition can be found in the notion of "social pacts" in Genovesi (2005[1765–1767], vol. I, ch 1) and in Filangieri (2003[1780], book III).
29 Consider, as seen, the various theories of intrinsic motivational crowding-out, beginning in economics with Frey (1997).
30 The verb "want" is used in the archaic sense of "lack" or "be short of."

31 Shortly before the historical building of the Archive was destroyed in the April 6 2009 earthquake, we had the chance to visit the Dragonetti-De Torres Archive at the National Archive of L'Aquila, where we found this and other private letters of Giacinto Dragonetti to his brother (the Archive has been rebuilt, and now the two letters and other material are available in the new building of the Archivio di Stato de L'Aquila, Bazzano via Galileo Galilei 1, Sez. Amministrativa, serie V, 42/1). Access to this material was made possible through the kind collaboration and support of Dr. Giovanna Lippi, who was in charge of the Dragonetti Archive and who was among the victims of the 2009 quake. To her goes our warmest remembrance.

32 On the issue of commerce as civilization in the eighteenth century, see also Bruni and Sugden (2000).

33 As showed in Bruni 2013, Genovesi in the latest part of his life (in his last edition of Lezioni) matured a less positive attitude towards commerce and his "spirit."

5 Facing crises

> Surely it is strange, too, to make the supremely happy man a solitary, for no one would choose the whole world on condition of being alone, since man is a political creature and one whose nature is to live with others ... Therefore the happy man needs friends.
>
> (Aristotle, *Nicomachean Ethics*)

Exit and voice

We are getting deeper into the dynamics characterizing VBOs. In the previous chapter, we analyzed the process of recruitment of workers who feel the VBO's mission as their own and its specific activity as a personal "vocation." We have left this topic open. In the present chapter (that can be seen as the "core" of our study), we ask ourselves what happens when some of these "Socrates" leave the VBO as a result of an internal crisis that has not been overcome, of an intergenerational change or any other reason related to a "symbolic" or "ideal" crisis of the organization.

These moments of crisis are important passages in every organization but they are absolutely crucial in VBOs. In particular, we shall examine the *mechanism* that can lead the intrinsically motivated people, those who have "vocation" and are the more interested in the mission of the organization, to abandon the organization when they perceive that their voice is ignored. We will see that the ideally motivated people – those, therefore, most concerned with the dimension of "vocation" – are affected first and more intensely by ideal crises. For this reason, if no heed is paid to their protest ("voice"), the crisis can make them abandon ("exit") the organization, making it fall in the death trap of the *cumulative mechanisms triggered.*[1]

The analysis is twofold: first, we combine the "Exit and Voice" model with some "critical mass" theories; and then we apply this combined model to VBOs.

This and the following chapter are a theoretical investigation of the dynamics that can arise in moments of crisis in VBOs. Further empirical research would be welcomed in order to verify the theoretical insights, in particular with respect to "critical mass" and imitation phenomena. In fact, while there exists a large body of empirical evidence about the importance of critical mass in organizations and their dynamics of change, empirical studies on the cumulative mechanisms of quality deterioration in moments of crisis and on the best practices of those organizations who have managed to solve successfully such crises are needed. We are convinced that the field of social economy could be extremely promising for such empirical analysis that, we hope, can soon become the research project of ourselves and of others.

The civil value of (good) voice

We begin this chapter with the following hypothesis: within VBOs there are group dynamics in which motivated minorities and the imitation effects of their actions have a key role. We claim that a few intrinsically motivated people determine the general cooperative (or non-cooperative) culture within organizations, especially in VBOs. For this reason, holding onto key members is crucial.

Our analytical starting point is the essay "Exit, Voice and Loyalty" by Albert O. Hirschman (1970) – a work whose theoretical potential, in particular in the analysis of VBOs, according to us, should be still discovered.[2]

In his book, Hirschman proposes to mix further the *exit* and *voice* instruments. *Voice* has not been traditionally taken into consideration in the market where consumers can "*exit*" whenever they do not like a particular commodity. In politics, where it is very difficult to *exit* (it is not easy, in fact, to go out of a political party, state or municipality in which one lives), *voice* becomes instead the main means to obtain changes.[3]

From the classical perspective, thus, there is almost no sense in protesting against Fiat because one does not like its cars. In this case it is convenient and sufficient to "exit" and purchase a different brand of car. Companies do not like the protest option (*voice*) since the *exit* one is easier and less expensive. Hirschman claims, instead, that more *exit* should be brought into politics and more *voice* on the market—a lesson that history has forced us to learn. When critical consumption movements today protest against and boycott a certain company, they show us how insufficient the *exit* of the market can be. Even though I decide to *exit*, other consumers remain and, therefore, the enterprise continues to pollute the natural and the social environment. Therefore, the *voice* option on the market directly concerns the exercise of citizenship and responsibility.

An important point of Hirschman's analysis consists in the "speculative" operations on markets based on *quality* rather than on *price* competition.

The classical example in this regard is the school. In the U.S. during the 1960s, there was a discussion about Milton Friedman's proposal to introduce vouchers into the educational system. According to Friedman, in financing education (a typical merit good that, thus, has to be subsidized) instead of intervening on the side of *supply* (through different kinds of economic aid assigned to schools), the government had to intervene directly on the side of *demand* by giving vouchers to students' parents. In this way, parents would have the possibility to spend the voucher received in whatever school they considered best for their children. Therefore, they would be *free to choose* as sustained by the famous social philosophy line of the Chicago school.[4] In this way, the vouchers' mechanism would increase competition and, as a consequence, also scholar services' efficiency and education's quality in the U.S. As a matter of fact, vouchers give families the *exit* option that serves as a tool of integration of the market mechanism into educational management. Whenever families do not like the service, they can choose the *exit* option. Hence, it gives the organization a signal to improve the quality of its services in order not to lose its clients and be "thrown out" of the market in the long run and enhances the rise of efficiency and, thus, social well-being.

According to Hirschman, the vouchers' introduction creates a typical case of *quality competition*. He does not deny that in certain circumstances the voucher system might function well (especially in highly inefficient and inflexible contexts in which a protest not accompanied by the threat of *exit* has no efficacy in obtaining an improvement). However, Hirschman seeks to "complicate" the economic discourse and, thus, adds some observations extremely important for VBOs also.

The starting point of Hirschman's analysis consists of realizing that in the case of quality competition, the market works in a fundamentally different way than in the classic case of *price competition* (in regard to which the market mechanisms have been designed and studied). In fact, the market and its mechanisms are not a good instrument in case of quality competition. Why? In mainstream economics, consumer demand is a function that links quantity (x) and price ($p(x)$) of a certain good or service. A change in quality is thus considered to be similar to a change in price:

> [A]n article of poor quality can often be considered to be simply less in quantity than the same article of standard quality; this is the case, for example, of the automobile tire which lasts on the average only half as long, in terms of mileage, as a high quality tire.
>
> (Hirschman 1970, p. 44)

Therefore, neoclassical economics considers quality competition a particular type of the more general price competition. Quality and price competition are, thus, seen as similar phenomena.[5]

One of Hirschman's main messages is, instead, that there are snares hidden in this non-distinction. In fact, in the traditional analysis of competition, when price rises, the marginal consumer who exits from the market is the one who, so to speak, "cares less" about that specific good, that is the person who has the lowest reservation price.[6] So, the consumer who exits the market for a particular commodity, can be defined the "worst," in the sense that she does not value that commodity as much as do other consumers.

In price competition consumers can be sorted in descending order according to their reservations price.

Suppose, as an example, that in a given market three types of consumers are present: A, with the highest reservation price (20), B (15) and C (10). At a market price 10, all three consumers would purchase the commodity. When the market price rises (i.e. from 10 to 12), quality being equal, consumer C—the "worst" one who has the lowest reservation price—will be the first one who leaves the market. B and A, who have relatively greater appreciation for that good due to their higher reservation prices, will instead remain in the market. In this case, the rise in price is similar to raising the bar in a high-jump event: those who remain in the competition are the best (unless doping or corrupt judges are involved) (see Figure 5.1).

For these same reasons, economists normally see the market mechanism based on price as a tool which guarantees the efficiency of the economic (and social) system. By choosing the "exit" option, consumers orient the

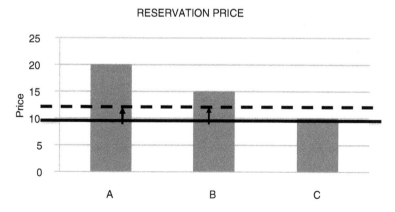

Figure 5.1 Price competition

market dynamics according to their preferences. The exit of consumers from the market is an inexpensive and flexible signal that allows companies to become more efficient. Moreover, economic theory normally recommends elastic demand: the faster the reaction of the demand to a variation in price, the more efficient is the market. For this reason, economic theory eyes with suspicion the consumers' complaints ("voice" in Hirschman's words) because they create friction within the efficient market mechanisms—since they require time, make demand inelastic and raise transaction costs. The use of the "exit" option, instead, increases efficiency (if the various assumptions in regard to competition are met).

What about the case of quality competition?

First of all, Hirschman reminds us that quality is a multidimensional concept. As previously mentioned, for many market goods, there is no significant distinction between price and quality in terms of competition and efficiency. There is, however, a kind (or dimension) of quality that, according to Hirschman, operates in an antipodal fashion with respect to standard competition. It is the case in which quality is not an objective and fully observable characteristic of a good, but rather a quality associated with the intrinsic dimensions of that particular good.

Hirschman claims correctly, that in such cases it is possible that the opposite effect in respect to the case of price competition occurs: in the event of a deterioration of quality, price being equal, the subject (A) who tends to exit first could be the "best" one, the one most sensitive to quality. In this scenario, the consumer normally does not correspond to the marginal consumer who exits in the event of a rise in price.

That is because the deterioration in quality is "frequently different for different customers of the article because appreciation of quality differs widely among them" (Hirschman 1982[1970], p. 48).

In this type of competition therefore, the customers' order could be reversed (as shown in Figure 5.2): the subject who reacts first to a deterioration in quality is the same one who values it highly.[7]

If, in fact, the quality drops, it could mean that for A (the best in this market) the quality drop "is equivalent to an increase in price that wipes out his entire consumer surplus" (ibid., p. 138), whereas for C "the equivalent price increase may be so small that he remains in the market" (ibid.).

Hence, when a drop in quality occurs, consumer A will be the first who threatens to leave the market. For her, in fact, a little deterioration of quality corresponds to an increase in price that nullifies her entire surplus. Therefore, the marginal consumer, from the point of view of price becomes "the most intra-marginal consumer in the case of quality deterioration" (ibid.). In other words, the person most interested in this kind of quality is not very interested in price (or less than the other consumers), given that the quality remains high.

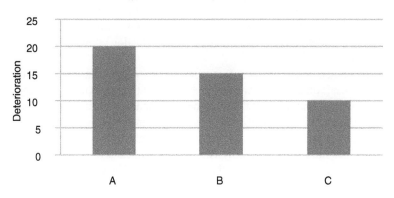

Figure 5.2 Quality deterioration

It is important to note that this analysis based on the distinction between price and quality competition is not suitable for all kinds of goods. Hirschman limits the analysis to the so-called "connoisseur goods" which have two main features (that are necessary conditions for the application of his and of our model): (1) the price-increase equivalents into which a quality decline can be translated are different for different consumers; (2) such equivalents are positively correlated with the corresponding consumer surpluses.

A typical example comes from the market for quality wine. The "best consumers" (those who more greatly appreciate the wine, i.e. who have the highest reservation price) are not very reactive to an increase of price given the high level of quality. If, instead, the wine (such as a Chianti from a particular area in Tuscany) loses quality, these same consumers are the first who tend to abandon the good.

Let us return to the example of vouchers. If a drop in quality causes the "exit" of the most sensitive parents (who will choose schools of better quality), the result could be a continuous deterioration of the school's level of quality because the supply might be recalibrated on the basis of the lowest standards of those who remain.[8]

In light of the above analysis, it is easier to grasp how this model fits in with the dynamics of VBOs. We think, in particular, of an Economy of Communion enterprise, a social cooperative or a fair trade shop that, at a certain point of their existence go through a deterioration in the motivational quality of their managers and, therefore, a deterioration in the ideal quality of the organization. The most common case of such a situation is the passage from the first stage of foundation of the organization to the second stage of institutionalization and normalization of its activity. Sometimes this transition might overlap with its founders' ageing and the need of an inter-generational change. In this case it is possible—and there is a lot of historical evidence to prove it—that a conflict situation within the organization occurs.

Hirschman's model tells us that in such cases we enter into a situation in which (ideal) quality is deteriorating. According to him, in fact, in this case "quality deterioration must therefore be redefined in subjective terms: from the members' viewpoint, it is equivalent to increasing disagreement with the organization's policies" (ibid., p. 87). In light of this theory, in what follows we hold that the quality conscious members will be first to voice when they see a deterioration of the VBO values and its ideal quality ("ideal quality" corresponds to the "connoisseur good" in Hirschman's definition). Ideal quality, in fact, respects the two key characteristics of the connoisseur good: a) the "price increase equivalent" is different for different people (intrinsically and not intrinsically motivated); b) the first to react (A) to an ideal quality deterioration are those with the higher consumer surplus in terms of price (the intrinsically motivated people are the least sensitive to variations in price—effort, wage, etc.—but the most sensitive to ideal quality deterioration.

It is the case, for example, of ideological consumers or investors who are prone to pay a higher price (or to earn a lower interest rate or not to have an ATM near to their homes) when the conditions that the organization they support by their choices are ethical and responsible. It is also the case of citizens who are willing to move a greater distance in order to buy fair trade products weekly from one particular shop because of its ideal quality. At the same time, these people are the first who voice and threaten to exit in case of deterioration of the ethical quality of products and/or the organization.

In the next chapter, we will examine some important consequences to the organizations that this possible "exit" of those who protest against the ideal quality deterioration may cause.

Notes

1 Moreover, the deterioration of its ideal quality damages also the competitive and development capacities of the organization facing the market demand. We should notice that intrinsic motivations' deterioration have an indirect effect on clients, even though they might not directly affect them. In other words, the negative effects of intrinsic motivation's deterioration do not depend on the weakening of clients' ideal awareness (we should not think that the patient of a social cooperative has to be intrinsically motivated when choosing it). However, some clients "demand" such ideal motivation from the organization and, in case they do not find it, are ready, ceteris paribus, to "exit."

2 There was much enthusiasm for Hirschman's book when it was first published, but after a few years the enthusiasm waned to the point that, in the last two decades, his work has seldom been spoken of in economics. To the best of our knowledge, his model has never been applied to VBOs. It is therefore worth re-examining this small but inspiring book and retracing his line of argument in order to analyze the object of our study.

3 *Exit Voice and Loyalty* was a successful book, but more among political scientists or sociologists than among economists, although Hirschman made a great analytical effort in writing the essay in the language of economics. But the kind of reasoning Hirschman was using in this book—and also in the *Strategy of Economic Development*, that was considered an heterodox book just because its methodology was based on psychological and subjective elements—was too far from neoclassical economics, in that time fully occupied by general equilibrium analysis (and in Europe by Sraffa's criticism) for understanding the message of *Exit Voice and Loyalty*, a book that however continues to inspire papers and researches, even among economists. A destiny somehow similar to that of James Dusenberry who developed a theory of consumption not less appealing and empirically relevant than those of Modigliani or Friedman, but much less successful in the discipline, because of its mixture of economic and sociological elements.

4 Friedman had criticized, among other things, free public schools (especially universities). His criticism rested on the assumption that "no meal is free" since "free" schools are actually paid with citizens' taxes. Therefore, a paradoxical situation occurs: the "black" (poor) pay a great part of the cost of "white's" (rich) children's education. Taxes, in fact, used to be paid essentially by employees whose children normally did not have access to the universities. According to Friedman, the children of entrepreneurs and professionals paying less taxes, were those who attended universities instead. The U.S. university system was, thus, de facto an iniquitous one in which the poor paid for the rich to go to school. A similar criticism is still addressed today by those liberal economists who criticize the public funding of theaters. They claim that wealthy people are the real beneficiaries of these merit goods, while employees who go to the theater very rarely are the ones who contribute the most. Obviously, such an issue is extremely complicated (the public benefits deriving from theaters and culture go far beyond their direct "consumers") and no conclusion can be made in such a brief note.

5 According to mainstream economics, if two commodities, A and B, have the same price, and one of them (A) is of higher quality Qa than the other (Qa>Qb), it is possible to identify two bundles of goods (one that consists of the A commodity, and one that consists of a hypothetic A commodity whose price and quality are lower) between which a consumer is indifferent.

6 The reservation price is the highest price at which a consumer would be willing to buy a certain commodity. Reservation price is linked to consumers' preferences and does not depend on income (which is a constraint on which consumers' choices also depend).

7 The reservation quality shows the highest tolerance in terms of deterioration of quality: customer A, whose reservation quality is equal to 10, is more sensible to quality deterioration than customer B, whose reservation quality is equal to 15.

8 In this case there would be a strong polarization: on the one hand, a few elite schools, and on the other, a large number of mediocre schools. A cost-benefit analysis would show a net loss of efficiency, measured on the basis of quality.

6 All equal, all different

The best way to understand the emergence of fashion trends, the ebb and flow of crime waves, or, for that matter, the transformation of unknown books into bestsellers, or the rise of teenage smoking ... is to think of them as epidemics.

(Malcolm Gladwell, *The Tipping Point*)

Critical mass

In the following pages, we shall discuss further the rich and complex argument presented in the previous chapter. Nevertheless, we shall base our analysis on a simple and, we believe, intuitive model.

The application of what we have been examining up to now, and thus the "exit" of the most motivated individuals, is quite immediate.

If an organization had to face the market demand (as in the case of social society organizations and different types of social enterprises), the deterioration of its ideal quality would have immediate negative consequences in terms of ability to keep its best clients (the ones most sensitive to the ideal quality of the organization). The ideal mission of the organization has a great deal to do with its success: it attracts consumers and sponsors who assign a social value to it as well as the creation of positive externalities. A deterioration of its members' motivation threatens that exactly the "best" clients abandon the organization.

Moreover, in times of crisis of its ideal quality (i.e. as in the case of a dimensional growth that makes it necessary to look for new managers, more efficient and prepared, but less motivated), the organization tends to lose its most motivated members. In addition to the previous phenomenon discussed, this one can be seen as even more alarming.

As a matter of fact, if a sufficient number of motivated workers were present within a VBO, they would have a spillover effect on the others. The rest of the workers, indeed, might start to imitate the motivated ones by working more and in a better way, by bringing "gratuity" to the "non-contractible" dimensions of its activity.[1] We might call this phenomenon "culture of the organization." However, created mainly by the most motivated individuals (for instance, the founders of the activity), it finally penetrates at different levels the way of acting of all the other members of the organization. It is worth noting that this "surplus" consequence due to the climate within VBOs and of their members' efforts (that, as in the case of Levi's "straight wall," serves as a motivation to do one's job well even without being controlled) has the characteristics of a public good whose existence is possible only if there is a sufficient number of people who contribute to it.

Our theoretical hypothesis, thus, is the following: the presence of intrinsically motivated people in a VBO is important not only because these people directly contribute to and preserve the "ideal quality" of the organization, but their presence indirectly influences the behavior of other workers via "exampling" which leads to imitation.

In order to develop this aspect of our analysis, we make use of "critical mass" models, specifically the versions developed by Schelling (1978) and Granovetter (1978). In other studies, these models have been utilized in order to explain some phenomena of collective behavior (such as riots or strikes, diffusion of innovations and fashion tendencies, cultural evolution) in which chain reaction mechanisms are triggered after overcoming a certain threshold or critical mass.[2] Moreover, history is full of examples (from Christianity to Gandhi's independence movement, from environmental to human rights' organizations) where significant cultural changes have been generated by the action of only a few intrinsically motivated people.

Gladwell (2002), for example, shows convincing evidence that a few people with particular features are sufficient to change broad-based situations.[3] He calls this phenomenon "the law of the few." According to such a theory, the culture of a given community or group does not depend on great numbers or on the "majority." It depends, rather, on a few members who are able to activate the imitators, who constitute the majority of the members of a community or of an organization. We can recognize here the ancient logic of the "yeast."

In this chapter, we shall extend this law of the few to organizations' internal dynamics, on the basis of the assumption that the "organizational culture" is determined mainly by "prophetic minorities" and afterwards, as a consequence of imitation processes, influences the behavior of all the members in the organization. That is, when a sufficient number of intrinsically motivated people are present in a VBO, their presence and culture influences other members improving their cooperative behavior.[4] In particular, we shall discuss what happens, according to such a theoretical perspective, when some of these core members abandon the organization, since this can trigger some forms of "poverty trap," in which the VBO might fall without realizing it straightaway.

Prophetic minorities and imitators

Our underlying hypothesis is common in organizational theory: an organization develops and grows when a cooperative attitude arises among the greatest part of its members that see more saliently the common good rather than individual interest; conversely, an organization tends to decline when the members look for individual gain over the common good.[5] In a VBO, we consider "cooperation" to be a kind of behavior which exceeds the contract terms and is somehow expressed in the adoption as one's own of the organization's values. In this way, it implies going beyond the specific tasks and duties required by the job description.

In our analysis we assume, paralleling Schelling's (1978) model, that in a given VBO there are three categories of members:

- GROUP I consists of the intrinsically motivated, those who cooperate regardless of other people's behavior because they get an intrinsic reward from the activity itself.[6] Such members have a second level of conditionality: *they cooperate if the VBO's ideal quality level is kept at a standard that for them is high "enough"*; otherwise, they tend to leave.

- GROUP II consists of members who never cooperate no matter how many other people cooperate within the organization. Their behavior is not influenced by that of others. This does not mean that such members are bad people but that, in a given organization, they simply do not ever exceed the contractual terms as defined. For these employees there is no difference between working for a VBO, a public enterprise or a multinational; they do not cooperate to an extent greater than the one required by contract and conventions. It is possible also that these workers turn out to be opportunistic and sly (and in real-life usually are) but such a negative ethical evaluation is not necessary so that a member of the organization is considered part of Group II. It is, instead, sufficient that a person does not do anything in order to exceed the contractual terms.

- GROUP III, which is usually the most numerous one, comprises the imitators, members who are between Group I and Group II since they are neither unconditional cooperators nor unconditional non-cooperators, but have the characteristic of cooperating if they see enough other members cooperating (and of not cooperating, otherwise). The interpretation of this "enough" is a key element in the functioning of our model since, as we will see further on, all members of Group III have their own measure of "enough," and when that measure is reached they will start to cooperate. Each member, however, has her own value: for

Andrea "enough" would be to see six people cooperating, for Maria— 12, for Georgia—two and so on. All of them (Andrea, Maria and Georgia), however, belong to this intermediate group of conditional cooperators.

We should note, then, that a wide interpretation of this threshold value ("enough") according to "how many other members cooperate," is needed. In real organizations people do or do not cooperate due to different types of reasons. According to us, however, in such cases relationships with others are a fundamental element. Normally people, especially when young, are very flexible to learn and change. The quality of their effort within an organization depends to a great extent on the role models they encounter. If in the office where I work I was surrounded by ten people, eight among whom behave in an opportunistic way, it would be highly probable that the quality of my work differs from the one expected in case there were only two opportunists. At the same time, our personal story, education and character play a crucial role: some of us have great difficulty in changing our behavior and need more time in order to do so (both when good or bad behaviors are concerned). On the other hand, there are some people who start to cooperate more quickly. Therefore, the meaning of these threshold values and "how many cooperators do we see around ourselves" should be interpreted in this broader sense which involves not employees only but also clients, suppliers and stakeholders. Generally speaking, a social enterprise or a VBO develops a cooperative culture able to face the future when it manages to activate in a positive way workers, sponsors, civil society and politics. Our intuition is that, even though extending the concept of "member" from employee to stakeholders in general, it is still possible to classify people according to these three different typologies and that the activation of cooperative behaviors is always a matter of human relations and imitation.

Hereinafter, we shall discuss mostly the case of employees and the internal dynamics of VBOs. However, it is useful to keep in mind this methodological clarification in order not to reduce the scope of the following pages.

Returning to the three types of groups presented above, we shall say that our triple distinction is consistent with the work of the English philosopher Martin Hollis (1998) on the topic of free donation of blood:

> There may well be some altruists who give their blood regardless and would do so as readily if the scheme were world-wide. There may also be some psychological egoists seeking the social approval gained by a display of public spirit. I suggest only that there is a group of donors whose creative altruism is local and conditional, a matter of there being

enough members for a joint undertaking. For persons who flourish in networks, generalised reciprocity is a rational expression of who they are and where they belong.

(Hollis 1998, p 147)

We call this level of "enough," this minimum number or proportion, threshold value of the activation of an individual. Since each agent of the group has a different threshold value, a frequency distribution of thresholds as well as a cumulative one exists. This cumulative distribution $(F(x))$ measures, for any number of workers x who are motivated, the number or proportion of workers for whom that number is "large enough" in order to start to cooperate.

Thus, if m represents the number of workers who cooperate in a period t, the number of people who will perform cooperatively in $t+1$ is given by $F(m)$. The equilibrium condition is therefore the following:

$$F(m^*) = m^*$$

Graphically, if we put m on the x-axis and $F(m)$ on the y-axis, the equilibrium points are those where the cumulative distribution function (c.d.f.) crosses the 45° line along which the values of the x- and y-axes are equal and, thus, cooperators will not tend to increase or diminish within time, as shown in Figure 6.1.

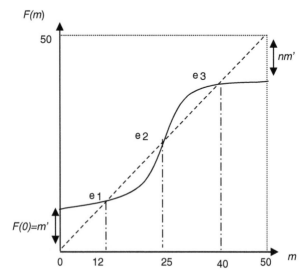

Figure 6.1 Threshold model

The *F(m)* function varies according to the distribution of the threshold values of the members of a given organization or community. The one represented in Figure 6.1 is based on a unimodal distribution of the threshold values (for example, the normal distribution which is the most common one: a bell-shaped distribution where the greater part of values is concentrated around the average).

The proportion of people whose threshold value equals 0 is given by the value of the $F(0)$ function, thus, in the graphic above, by the starting point of the *y*-axis of the cumulative function. If $F(0) = 0$ there are no intrinsically motivated workers, members of Group I (people who continue to cooperate even when nobody else, except themselves, do so) within the organization.

We can also read the graphic dynamically. In this case, on the *x*-axis we see the number of people who cooperate today[7]; on the *y*-axis, instead, the distribution shows the ones who will cooperate tomorrow (according to the threshold value).[8] In such a context, a point of equilibrium (if stable) is a point in which the number of the ones who cooperate today equals the number of individuals who will cooperate tomorrow: no shift away from this equilibrium is possible unless external disruption occurs.

For example, if three individuals within the organization had a threshold value equal to 2 and one a threshold equal to 3, and moreover we could observe three motivated workers today, there would be four more (3+1) individuals willing to cooperate in the next period, and so on. We are in an equilibrium point whenever the number of people who are motivated today equals the number of people who will be motivated tomorrow (where the $F(x)$ function intersects the 45° axis).

As we can see in the graphic, depending on the threshold values' distribution (and, thus, the shape of the cumulative function $F(x)$), there might be more than one equilibrium point possible. At the same time, it is also possible that there is only one equilibrium point or that no equilibrium different from 0 exists (when the cumulative distribution function lies below the 45° line). This last case occurs when there are no workers from Group I (whose threshold value equals 0), when there is no one who begins to cooperate without seeing someone else do it.

However, more interesting are the cases, such as the one shown in Figure 6.1, in which there are multiple equilibrium points. In the graphic we find three equilibria: two stable (e_1 and e_3) and one unstable (e_2). Therefore, according to the initial conditions, along the same distribution of threshold values both a situation of high-level or low-level cooperation equilibrium may occur: if in the initial stage of the process the number of motivated workers is greater than the "critical mass" (which in the graphic is represented by the e_2 value on the *x*-axis 25) with the passage of time a convergence towards the high-level cooperation equilibrium (e_3) will occur; otherwise the low-level one (e_1) will predominate.

We now take into consideration the same example used by Schelling (1978) that deals with a university optional seminar. There are a 100 students who might attend the seminar. Schelling's starting question is: why in some years the number of students attending does not diminish or even grows after the first lecture, while in others the number of students attending the same seminar (held by the same professor) tends to decrease drastically after the first lecture)?

Schelling's hypothesis of the process' underlying dynamics is as follows. An x percentage of the students attend the seminar during the first day; from the second day, this percentage will diminish or increase depending on two factors: on one hand, how many students abandon the seminar after the first day and, on the other, what are the students' threshold values, thus, how many classmates does each student want to see attending the seminar in order to decide herself to continue attending (the shape of the cumulative function $F(x)$ depends exactly on these values). In fact, if during the first day only a few students attend the class and the threshold values are low, the number of students attending will probably decrease over time: why? Those students who have participated today and whose threshold value is slightly higher than the number of the participants, will not come again tomorrow. Therefore, the "marginal" participants who would continue to come only if the number of students attending the class during the first day is equal to the number of the participants during the second day, will not come in the third day. As a result, a cumulative process is triggered.

Referring to the graphic we might say that, in the case of such dynamics, the significant part of the curve lies below the 45° line (and, thus, will converge over time towards the low-level equilibrium e_1).

If, instead, in t=1 the number of students attending the seminar is greater than the number of students expected (the "critical mass" is exceeded during the first day and, thus, the significant part of the curve lies above the 45° line), the number of students will tend to increase over time (this is the exact reason why only e_1 and e_3 are stable equilibria and e_2 is not).[9]

When motivated minorities are really important

A field in which critical mass models might be applied is the one concerning the ecological culture or its related activities such as the recycling of waste. Without taking into consideration the various types of legislation or incentive and sanction mechanisms applied in different countries, we ask ourselves how is it possible that the ecological culture and environmental behavior differ so much between and even within the same country. Also in this case, we might use the critical mass theory (and threshold values) in order to explain such phenomena. Whenever, for example, in a given society there is neither an "élite" of unconditional cooperators (people who have an ecological culture) who might play the role of *starters* of the process, nor a civic culture inclined to cooperation in the field of ecology—and thus the threshold values of citizens are low—spontaneous processes of cooperation and recycling do not ever start and the only possible equilibrium is in the 0 point.

If the ecological culture within a given society is low, instead, (and, therefore, the threshold values are very high: I need to see many people doing the waste sorting before I start doing it myself) but at the same time there is a small group of unconditional cooperators (Group I), it is possible to reach a number of cooperators greater than 0, although not a big one. Such is the case of the "niche" when the ecological culture remains confined in a niche almost exclusively composed of intrinsically motivated people (Group I) and just a few imitators (Group III). This small niche of cooperators lasts over time and does return to the starting 0 point. But such an élite is not capable of transforming the entire culture of the population.

Finally, when ecological culture is spread among citizens and, thus, their threshold values are not too high[10] and, as in the case shown in the graphic, there are enough unconditional cooperators (Group I), it is possible that a high-level equilibrium in which almost the entire population would do the waste sorting is reached.

Going back to our model, the selection of a low or high-level equilibrium and, thus, the success or failure of an ecological or cultural campaign, or of an organizational change depends on several factors:

- the number of intrinsically motivated people (the size of Group I);
- the distribution of thresholds among the people of Group III (and, thus, the shape of the cumulative function $F(x)$), whose imitating behavior depends on how many cooperators are present; and
- the number of non intrinsically-motivated people (the size of Group II whose members' threshold values is infinite).

Let us now look at another example. Let us suppose that an important international organization decides to start an environmental campaign in the cities of Archimedes and Erasmus, which are situated in two different countries. The campaign's objective is to clean up a park with daily interventions over an entire month. The promotional campaign applied is the same. Let us, then, suppose that the organization manages to start up the campaign with the same percentage of people (25 percent, for example) both in the city of Archimedes and Erasmus. What would the critical mass model suggest in this case? Simply that the success of the campaign could be quite different in the two cities depending on the threshold values of their population (and, thus, the shape of the cumulative function): in Erasmus 25 percent of the population might be enough to exceed the critical mass, but in Archimedes where threshold values are higher, things might be quite different and citizens might not spring into action (the campaign does not succeed: after the first day the number of participants starts to decline until it reaches the point where only the volunteers of the organization, members of Group I, as well as a few imitators go to the park).

All of this suggests that the presence of some highly motivated individuals is not always enough to trigger the cooperative culture within an organization: much depends on the average culture of its workers. Therefore, there is no guarantee that a successful social enterprise in a certain region would also be successful in another one even though its promoters, techniques and organizational forms are all the same. The success of any cooperative action depends largely on people and their culture as well as on what happens during the first day: a great part of the success of any initiative depends on its launch, on the first day of its action.

However, it is still true that a key factor in the dynamics of this process is the number of intrinsically motivated people (the "core members").[11]

In the next section, we will discuss what would happen if some changes within the organization reduce the number of these "core members" since, as we have already seen in the previous chapter, some members of Group I choose the *exit* option.

Some possible scenarios (and some notes of caution for managers)

Let us now go back to the *exit* and *voice* theory. As we have already seen, if there is no possibility of a *voice*, the most intrinsically motivated people are the first ones who threaten to leave. If some of the most motivated people (of Group I) leave the organization because they have no voice in it, the effect on people whose behavior depends on how many motivated workers exist in the VBO (those belonging to Group III) could be substantial. In the worst of cases, the high equilibrium point could even be destroyed as a consequence of the exit of some intrinsically motivated people (Group I). There are 50 people working in the VBO in Figure 6.1. Ten of them (indicated by the m segment on the vertical axis in the graph) are intrinsically motivated (Group I) and about 10 (the nm segment) are not (Group II). All other workers (about 30) are "imitators" (Group III). Two stable equilibria exist (12 [e_1] and 40 [e_3] workers): depending on the initial conditions and on the exceeding of the critical mass in the beginning of the process. However, three equilibria in total are possible (two stable and one unstable), but there are also other cases, as the one presented in Figure 6.2 where there is a single equilibrium point or an equilibrium point does not even exist (or better, to be more precise, is equal to 0). It all depends on the distribution of the threshold values and, thus, on the "culture" of a given organization or community.

In this example, the A curve (shown in Figure 6.2) represents the case where only one (positive) equilibrium exists; the B curve, instead, represents the case where no equilibrium point in which the proportion of motivated workers within the organization is greater than 0 is possible. In this last case, there is no cooperation and, thus, the process never starts.

Therefore, the level of cooperation established within a VBO is closely related to the number of intrinsically motivated people. It, however, depends also on the threshold values' distribution of those workers whose conditional behavior is directly affected by the number of motivated people present. Moreover, a key factor is the presence of at least some intrinsically motivated people, without whom the process of cooperation just does not begin.

The presence of people belonging to Group I is, therefore, a necessary condition for the activation of the virtuous process: such is the main message that we have tried to emphasize until now. At the same time, the motivation of Group I members is not a *sufficient* condition for the long duration of the process and its stability during the inevitable periods of crisis. It is just a *necessary* condition instead. The threshold values' distribution and, thus, imitators play a crucial role too.

As a matter of fact, a VBO would be extremely vulnerable and fragile, if there were only a few imitators and a cooperative culture fails to take hold within the organization. A good *governance* should, on one hand, focus on the intrinsically motivated individuals "neglecting" all others. At the same time, however, it is also necessary to take care, cultivate and invest in the culture of those "intermediate" workers on whom, although conditional cooperators and imitators, the general culture of the VBO depends. If within the organization (as in the case represented by the A curve in Figure 6.2) there was a good number of individuals belonging to Group III whose threshold values are low (people who, thus, easily cooperate) this would make the organization less vulnerable in front of the crises and would be a precondition so that cooperation can be activated and maintained over time.

We shall now discuss what would happen within a VBO when it goes through an intergenerational or other kind of crisis which reduces the ideal quality of the organization. As we have already seen, if there is no possibility of a *voice*, the most intrinsically motivated people are the first who threaten to leave. We can ask ourselves why does this happen even though the most motivated individuals are those willing to carry on even alone (they are the ones who contribute to this specific type of public good called cooperative "climate" of the organization even when others do not do the same).

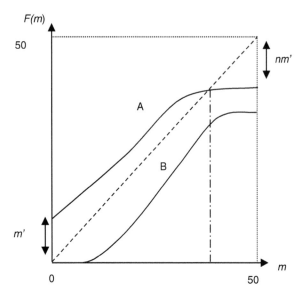

Figure 6.2 Single equilibrium or no equilibrium

It should be taken into consideration the fact that individuals belonging to Group I carry on even alone only *if and until* the VBO's ideal quality level remains and is by them considered high "enough."[12] Otherwise, they can no longer find the reason for their commitment. It is as if the intrinsically motivated individual had a psychological component integrated in her pay-off. A component which, when high enough, makes her cooperate unconditionally, although conscious of the possibility of free-riding of the non-motivated individuals also in her own regard. Such a value is not, however, a constant parameter but a variable which is influenced by the environment, and evolves and changes over time. In other words, it is as if the intrinsically motivated individuals had an "identity" or "ideal" constraint: if they see or think that the organization is losing its original ideal identity (because of the new management's culture, for example), this intrinsic component that has previously driven them during the years not to measure their commitment in the VBO, might sharply decline or even disappear.

What might the consequences be? First, this can make them *exit*, thus, leave the organization (for example, the founders who retire or leave). It is not, however, necessary that such an extreme consequence occurs. As a matter of fact, it is enough that the ideal crisis reduces their intrinsic value below a certain threshold making, this way, their cooperation conditional, rather than unconditional. According to our model, this would mean that the worker or / and shareholder moves from Group I to Group III and, thus, becomes a conditional cooperator. This would mean that, from now on, she would start to cooperate in dependence on the relative convenience shown by the cost/benefits analysis. Expressions such as "it is not worth it anymore" might signalize such transition from Group I to Group III.

If some of the most motivated people leave the organization (literally or turning into conditional cooperators), the effect on other members is substantial. As we can see in Figure 6.3, in the worst of cases, the high-equilibrium point where most of the members of the VBO are motivated might even disappear.

Let us suppose that during the first stage the VBO reaches an equilibrium point where a considerable number of cooperators are present within it (for example, 40). Let us also suppose that a motivational crisis lowers the ideal quality level of the organization driving some of the most motivated individuals and, thus, those most interested in the ideal quality, to leave the organization (or "switch allegiance from one group to another"). If the most motivated "leave" (literally or moving from one group to another and, thus, changing commitment) the threshold values' curve shifts downwards.[13]

In Figure 6.3, we show the case in which a few of the intrinsically motivated members (in our example, about six) leave the VBO: in this case it will not be possible to reach the high-level equilibrium where a large number of cooperators are present since such an equilibrium simply does not exist anymore. The *exit* of just five or six intrinsically motivated members

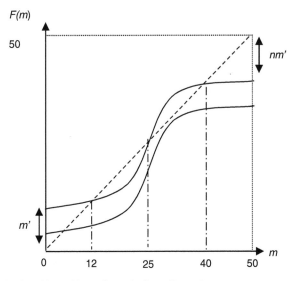

Figure 6.3 The effect of loss of people from Group I

leads to a new equilibrium point where we find only six or seven motivated workers, instead of 40 as in the previous situation! We think that such a result is quite important. The exit of a few intrinsically motivated individuals has an amplified impact on the dynamics within the organization.[14]

What we have discussed so far gives us the opportunity to reflect on some important aspects of the dynamic nature of motivations within organizations, especially within VBOs. The situations described above reveal one crucial dimension in the case when VBOs are concerned: if the founders or the intrinsically motivated members are a minority and want to create a strong organization able to withstand crises, they should not take into consideration their own motivations only (that are certainly crucial) and neglect those of the "intermediate" members or imitators (Group III). Whenever the cooperative culture of these individuals is low (and, thus, their threshold values are high), the VBO would be fragile and exposed to severe crises. In this case, there is the possibility that the retirement or *exit* of just a few members belonging to Group I causes the loss of the entire culture of the organization. Such are the cases of organizations—social cooperatives, family businesses, Economy of Communion enterprises, etc.—in which the exit of the founder provokes the decline or even disappearance of the original ideal culture.

An important historical example in this regard is the case of Adriano Olivetti who, with his personal charisma, founded one of the most innovative enterprises (from both a social and relational point of view) in the twentieth century. After his death, however, the experience of such a "community" enterprise did not last because of (even though not exclusively) the lack of a culture spread among a greater number of members of the organization and not only its founder and a few collaborators.

An enterprise would resist much better the shocks due to intergenerational changes or to the *exit* of intrinsically motivated people, when its founder(s) work to raise the general culture of the whole enterprise, at each level, and make it possible that all of its members somehow internalize this specific culture.

The A curve in Figure 6.4 illustrates the case in which a large number of individuals belonging to Group III (whose threshold values are low and cooperative behavior can be, thus, easily enabled) are present within the VBO. As we can see in the following graph, in such cases the *exit* of some of Group I's members might have significant but not devastating effects.

Also in this case a little reduction of the number of people belonging to Group I has important consequences, although not radical as in the previous one (in which the number of cooperators shrunk from 40 to seven only). All this suggests how important it is within a VBO to take into consideration not only the members of Group I but also those of Group III. The presence

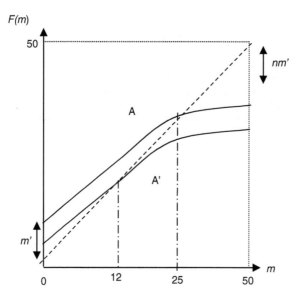

Figure 6.4 Group III with low threshold

of people belonging to Group III, especially the ones whose threshold values are low (people who would, thus, start to cooperate soon enough) makes it easier to deal with generational changes and restrict the negative effects in times of crisis.

If the organization considers only the members of Group I, instead, cares about and invests only in this "élite" of motivated people, it would be possible to reach a high-level equilibrium during some good periods, but the organization would become extremely fragile and exposed to catastrophes in the periods of crisis.

Notes

1 More recently Durlauf and other scholars have proposed a relevant formalization of critical mass models within their research project known as "social economics." These scholars found substantial empirical and historical evidence of collective behaviors that reflect the assumptions behind these critical mass models. For example, Durlauf (2001) analyzes the emergence of Silicon Valley, a phenomenon of diffusion of innovation and migration.
2 It is worth noting that the minority (the "few") is not necessarily an élite group. The model indicates nothing about the hierarchical role of the people who activate the organizational change.
3 But the key point is to discuss what sufficient number actually means. We use the concept of "sufficient number" in the sense of Schelling's theory of "critical

mass." In this approach, "sufficient" means the minimum number that can produce a chain reaction.

4 For a review of this literature, see for example, Astley and Van de Van (1983), Keley (1978) and Williamson (1995) as a classical broader text.

5 See Bruni and Smerilli (2004).

6 This interpretation reflects the approach of Granovetter, one of the pioneers in the application of critical mass models to various social phenomena (Granovetter-Soong 1983).

7 We have to remind ourselves that threshold values are not an invariable characteristic of individuals but rather change and evolve over time according to the culture of a given organization.

8 The e_2 point might be an equilibrium only in the case in which the whole process starts exactly at the point of this threshold value (in our example, 25). Otherwise, a convergence towards e_1 (if the threshold is not exceeded) or towards e_3 will occur.

9 We are reminded here that if a person has a high ecological value, her threshold value is low.

10 As already mentioned, the importance of intrinsic motivation has been underlined by other scholars, such as Frey, or Le Grand. In particular, Frey distinguishes between "intrinsic" and "extrinsic" motivations, whereas Le Grand differentiates between "knavish" and "knightly" ones. The purpose of both scholars is to design a good incentive scheme in order to keep "intrinsic" or "knavish" motivations high in workers. Our analysis of motivations in VBOs, instead, although sharing the basic tenets of these theories, emphasizes a different point, i.e. the relationship between those members who are intrinsically motivated (or "knightly" in Le Grand words) and other members (those in Group III) who are not fully intrinsically nor extrinsically motivated, but who, via imitation, play an important role in determining which equilibrium point (or "culture") will be reached in a given VBO.

11 As a matter of fact, the measure of enough also concerns the individuals from Group I. This is not, however, influenced by the level of others' cooperation, but rather by the ideal quality of the VBO: one might carry on irrespective of others' behavior but only until she feels it is worth it.

12 Certainly the starting point of the curve that lies on the y-axis is lower due to the lower number of people belonging to Group I. Afterwards, depending on whether an exit or motivational shift occurs (when people belonging to Group I move to Group III) the curve undergoes a downward shift or a change of its shape. On this we refer to Schelling (1978).

13 However, it is not always true that the high-level equilibrium (if it exists before the crisis) is destroyed, even though there is such a possibility.

14 We should not consider these "types" in a simplistic and, thus, wrong manner: in some dimensions of the life of a VBO, a certain type might perfectly correspond to the real person (for example, the founder). But normally in other kinds of dynamics, the three types coexist in the same person and predominate according to the specific context, mood or stage of life. It should not be assumed that the "nature" of the protest of people from Group I is always constructive and good.

7   The nature of voice

> When loyalty is present exit abruptly changes character: the applauded
> rational behavior of the alert consumer shifting to a better buy becomes
> disgraceful defection, desertion, and treason.
>
> (Hirschman, *Exit, Voice and Loyalty*)

"Good" and "bad" voice

What we have just discussed in the previous chapter has relevant consequences that we take into consideration in this chapter.

First, it is important to know how to identify from which of the three
groups (I, II or III) does the protest come. As a matter of fact, the protest
of the intrinsically motivated people (members of Group I) should be welcomed and always plays an important role. On one hand, it aims at the
recovery of the ideal quality of the organization. On the other, it produces
the effects already analyzed when it leads these members to *exit* the organization. The situation is different when those who protest are members of
Group II. In this case, the protest does not express the desire to recover
the ideal quality of the organization but is usually the fruit of selfish and
opportunistic interests instead. A careful management should be able to distinguish who the protest comes from and, hereafter, recognize whether such
a protest might be potentially constructive for the organization or not. These
two types of protest should be handled in a substantially different way: *a
crisis might also worsen when the management is not able to identify the
kind of protest deriving from within the VBO.* In such cases, attention is not
paid to the "good" protest but the organization rather devotes energy and
time to the "bad" and destructive one. Some enterprises become bankrupt
because they do not listen to the "good" protests, others because they do
listen to the "bad" ones.

There are some signals that help in identifying whether a protest is
"good" or not. First of all, protest should be public and transparent and not
a gossip or whisper along the corridors. The ancient adage which shows the

difference between a friend and an enemy is still true today: when you make a fault, friends tell you and enemies tell everyone else (in a non-public and transparent way). Moreover, the one who makes this "good" kind of protest, takes personally a risk and, thus, the responsibility for her own words and actions. Finally, the "good" *voice* is onerous for those who express it since it is never simply a request for change made to others but always directly involves a change and greater commitment also on the part of the ones who protest. We can be quite sure that when a protest is not public and transparent, when the ones protesting are not ready to pay in person but rather claims that only the others should change, it does not aim at restoring the lost ideal quality of the organization but at the satisfaction of certain personal interests instead. Such a kind of protest certainly comes from a person who puts her own needs and subjective views rather than the common good in the first place.

The ability to distinguish the different kinds of *voice*—a really hard task—is part of the art of managing such complex organizations as the ones analyzed here. It should be noted that good and bad protests might coexist in the same person. Therefore, we should not think of the distinction between the three types of members as a static and rigid one, but rather as a model: on some occasions real people behave as members of Group I, on others— of Group II or III.[1] Although a certain person can be generally described as type 1, it is possible that even the founder of the VBO's protest might sometimes be wrong and should not be accepted. Therefore, VBO managers should not consider the protest of certain people as always "good" and of others—as always wrong. The ability to avoid such kinds of mistakes is also a part of the art of managing a VBO.

Second, our model shows also that even when a VBO settles in the "cooperative" equilibrium point (in which the organization functions well and its culture is cooperative), there is still within it a certain number of non-cooperators. Therefore, we should not confuse the presence of a good cooperative culture with unanimity: organizations are dynamic and evolving organisms and it would be naïve to think that a 100 percent of a VBO's members have a cooperative attitude and to expect it. A good management should also know how to deal with this section of non-cooperators within the VBO without trying to convert them (also because these "non-cooperators" are not always the same people: some individuals behave as type III when they make certain decisions; others—when they make another kind of decision). A mistake, very common within organizations, should be avoided: to always listen to the protest of certain people only and never do so to the protest of others.

All this suggests that the *mysterium iniquitatis* really exists: organizations develop when, on one hand, they avoid the ever-present risk of being cynical and, thus, always see people as potentially opportunistic and knightly. On the other hand, they do not underestimate, because of irenicism, the presence of non-cooperative behaviors also within successful VBOs. Even in this favorable case there will always be someone who does not fully share the organization's culture and someone else whose behavior changes over time.

Loyalty

The above analysis shows that the disregard for the importance of intrinsically motivated people can generate some cumulative dynamics within the VBO. Such dynamics represent a sort of poverty trap.

In this regard, an important question arises: how to avoid these poverty traps?

What Hirschman suggests in such cases is "loyalty." However, in order to understand the role that "loyalty" plays, we should start one more time from the "voice" option. *Voice* is defined as:

> Any attempt at all to change, rather than to escape from, an objectionable state of affairs, whether through individual or collective petition to the management directly in charge, through appeal to a higher authority with the intention of forcing a change in management, or through various types of actions and protests, including those who are meant to mobilize public opinion.
>
> (Hirschman 1970, p. 30)

In fact, in order to avoid losing core members, who are the first who threaten to leave the organization in the case of loss of quality, and having them select the "loyalty" option instead of the "exit" option, it is necessary that those members foresee "improvements to occur as a result of actions to be taken by himself or by others with him or just by others" (Hirschman 1970, p. 37).

When members (or stakeholders, such as financial supporters) are loyal, the voice option becomes an alternative to the exit option. The possibility of selecting the loyalty option by the intrinsically motivated members is, then, subordinated to the hope of recuperation of the lost ideal quality. Then, loyalty requires "listening" to voice: "the decision whether to exit will often be taken in the light of the prospects for the effective use of voice" (Hirschman 1970, p. 39).

In other words, exit is, for intrinsically motivated subjects, an extreme decision taken only when within the organization there is no more room for voice. Sometimes, the exit option is not the best choice, but rather a second one forced by the impossibility to foresee a hope of recuperation of the lost ideal quality because voice "has not been heard."

The loyalty of those who protest but do not leave helps the organization to avoid cumulative deterioration.

How, then, is loyalty fostered in organizations and specifically in VBOs?

Pluralistic and participative governance that gives room to voice fosters the intrinsically motivated people's hope of reviving that ideal quality that has diminished or been lost. This hope rekindles the sense of purpose in the intrinsically motivated people (Group I) and gives them a reason to continue their work within the VBO, i.e., giving room to voice overshadows the exit option, and may foster loyalty.

Thus, if what we have tried to argue in this chapter is true—if the key factor that determines the organizational culture is the retention of the intrinsically motivated people—then the most important art for managers of VBOs becomes the art of listening to the voice of those intrinsically motivated people concerned with deterioration of ideal quality of the organization and, therefore, make it possible for them to stay even when they feel such an ideal crisis. In this way, managers would avoid the triggering of cumulative processes of deterioration.

The important dialogue inside the organization

We need further considerations in order to further explore the relational and motivation dynamics inside organizations. First of all, it is important to be aware that the motivations to work vary through time. During the first years of a new career people are excited and enthusiastic. After 20 years in the same office of an organization, the enthusiasm dies out. Without new and more compelling motivations, workers become weary and cynical. Workplaces are filled with discontented middle-age workers. Much of the research done in this area reveals a U-shaped graph correlating happiness and age. The point of minimum happiness hits around 45 years of age. From this age, workers' happiness increases if they have good health and social relationships.

Labor regulations have ignored the different stages of human life. The 20-year-old Mary was a different worker from the one she is now in her 60s. Businesses do not follow people's natural aging process. Thus, when one has "journeyed half of our life's way" [Dante], one is trapped in both a professional and private mid-life crisis—labor is life.

Enterprises do not invest enough in relationships. In private or state-owned companies, workers are often regarded as selfish and untrustworthy, and bosses believe they have to control and reward employees to make them productive. This environment produces unhappiness—when will countries take quality of working life indicators seriously? Therefore, workers seek happiness outside their workplaces, spending lots of money on wellness centers and spas. Is this a wise and sustainable solution? Would it not be wiser to develop healthy relationships within workplaces and thereby increase workers' well-being?

It is not by chance that religious orders—typical VBOs—have built the longest lasting institutions in the Western world—an average Benedictine Abbey is five centuries old. Their old age and smooth operations flow from good governance. VBOs, but any organization, should implement a few of their regulations; religious orders' rules contain management teachings that are people-centered and universal.

For example, the members of a religious order periodically meet with their superior in private. This practice promotes healthy relationships within the organization, and it is particularly precious for listening to the voice, and, crucially, for distinguishing the good from the bad voices. Regrettably, employees of numerous enterprises—sometimes also VBOs—reach retirement having never talked privately to their bosses. In those few enterprises and cooperatives where such private meetings take place, they are few and irregular.

Today, more than ever, private talks between supervisors and workers—and not only the widespread practice of coaching—are vital. Regular private meetings (twice a year, for example) would benefit workers and organizations in many ways.

Employees and bosses should be able to privately express their complaints, hardships, misunderstandings and woes. Taking this action can help avoid gossip, rumors and grudges that end up having a destructive impact on corporate life. Since biblical times people have spread rumors, not only gossipmongers and defamers. However, protests, critics and complaints can be constructive if institutions use such information wisely. In the same way, gratitude is essential in every community and most effective when properly expressed.

Saying "thank you!," "good job!" or even "sorry" to an employee in the corridors or on the phone is not enough. These words are precious ones that should not be used lightly. Furthermore, one-on-one talks promote brotherhood rather than hierarchy; they increase *philia* among workers—those who partake in these conversations both listen and speak, give and receive. Executives will raise their game if they accept critiques from their subordinates and commit themselves to changing. Their biggest mistake in personal meetings is avoiding complaints by cutting off the employees ("you miss the point …," "you do not see the full picture …," "let me explain …").

In private conversations one should not have to justify oneself, but listen and welcome criticism and hardships—we are so undeveloped in the art of listening. A supervisor should listen, register and process critiques and not criticize in return. The employee has the right to complain, and the manager the duty to listen. Companies need to provide proper places and a schedule for private meetings. Workers and managers should also undertake ethical training to better take part in these. It is not easy to hold one-on-one meetings; businesses should work hard on this and learn from prior mistakes—if they do, the fruits will be abundant.

Employees' first and last private talks with their bosses are very important. Welcome interviews should include a presentation on the enterprise's traditions, history, goals and mission. Newly hired workers will have a chance to share their aspirations, passions and introduce themselves to the working community; everyone should celebrate their arrival.

The farewell meeting is equally important. Many times it concludes the best period of someone's life. It is a life changing event. One may say "thank you" or "sorry" and make this critical encounter spiritually fulfilling and meaningful.

The art of governance

As we have already said, when an organization manages to establish a pluralistic governance, when it "listens to" the good protests and does not marginalize the complex and uncomfortable issues that raise requests concerning its ideal quality, it is possible that *voice* does not lead to the exit but rather to the loyalty option. One signal of the ability to listen to the good *voice* is not to consider each person that raises similar kinds of objections as a maniac or a nuisance (although he may actually act like one). A VBO should foster the ability of its management to "cultivate" such kinds of "manias" because they usually conceal the possibility of future progress and the new ideal motivations that make a VBO "charismatic."

As a matter of fact, if the protest is "any attempt at all to change … an objectionable state of affairs" (Hirschman 1970, p. 30), then if the person that protests foresees the real possibility of a quality improvement, he may decide to stay. In this way, her protest turns into loyalty and strengthens the VBO. Loyalty, however, is very demanding since it requires the hope of the ones who protest that their requests will be heard: if they do not have hope, instead, the exit option might become the only possible alternative and trigger the kind of consequences already discussed.

In conclusion, we can say that VBOs live also and, to a certain extent mainly, due to the existence of intrinsic motivations: they are demanded by civil society, share and need holders and cannot be "purchased" on the labor market, but rather need to be selected through the use of indirect mechanisms. People embody motivations. But not all of them: only the ones who have a "motivation capital" built up over the years and even decades, capital for which there are no market substitutes.

In this chapter, we have looked at human motivations as a form of wealth, as a measure of the culture of any kind of human organization or community. Crises—whatever their nature might be—tend to diminish this "wealth" and provoke in this way the loss of freedoms. Crises become unbearable whenever they destroy the symbolic and identity capital of people and organizations that, especially in VBOs, cannot be offered either by loans or by state aids. We hope that, in a time of crisis like ours, the things suggested in this chapter might somehow help those people who live within the organizations have ideals, love the human passions and help them not lose their underestimation of these crises and conflicts.

Note

1 We should not consider these "types" in a simplistic and, thus, wrong manner: in some dimensions of the life of a VBO, a certain type might perfectly correspond to the real person (for example, the founder). But normally in other kinds of dynamics, the three types coexist in the same person and predominate according to the specific context, mood or stage of life. It should not be assumed that the "nature" of the protest of people from Group I is always constructive and good.

8 Semantics of the relationships within a VBO

Organizations as networks

> Today we increasingly recognize that nothing happens in isolation. Most events and phenomena are connected, caused by, and interacting with a huge number of other pieces of a complex universal puzzle. We have come to see that we live in a small world, where everything is linked to everything else ... We have come to grasp the importance of networks
>
> (A. Barabasi, *Linked*)

Introduction

The topics covered in the previous chapter introduce a reflection on organizations seen as networks. Workers are the nodes of these networks and are connected to each other by more or less strong links. As a matter of fact, life in common can be read as networks and links. Organizations themselves can be considered an example of a social network in which not only hierarchical and formal relationships matter but the links between their members beyond organization charts and tasks as well. Also the market, in its particular way, can be seen as one large and complex network. The study of organizations through the lens of networks will allow us to grasp some aspects related to the type of links established between the members of a VBO that might not be noticed right away. As one of the greatest scholars of networks underlines:

> We must remove the wrapping. The goal before us is to understand complexity. To achieve that, we must move beyond structure and topology and start focusing on the dynamics that take place between the links. Networks are only the skeletons of complexity, the highways for the various processes that make our world hum. To describe society, we must dress the links of the social network with actual dynamical interactions between people.
>
> (Barabasi 2005, p. 225)

We will discuss hereafter the different types of networks, the effects of incentives on people who play a specific role within them, as well as the relational goods that might evolve and spread in these networks over time. Relational goods are expressed mainly in the bonds between people that form an entire network of human relationships.

Links are the bonds that connect different people (the nodes of a network) within the organization (see Figure 8.1). They are the ways of disseminating information, new knowledge as well as imitation processes of cooperative behaviors: when there are many links which connect one person to the other members of the organization, the effect of her actions will also affect a large number of people.

In order to understand better the dynamics triggered during times of crisis, it could be useful not only to identify the different kinds of people working in a VBO, but analyze also the semantics of relationships between them. People who deal with management understand very well that the organization chart and the formal structure usually tells us little about the informal or substantial distribution of the centers of power and, especially, of leadership within the organization. Even when small groups are concerned, managers are often surprised by the paths of collaboration (which are different than the ones imagined when roles and hierarchies were established) and the ones suggested, instead, by the organization chart.[1] In order to give an example, we show in the following figures both the organization chart and an analysis of how the organization's relationship network is actually composed. The grammar (the organization chart) does not correspond to the semantics of relationships within a community or an organization, especially when it comes to complex realities.

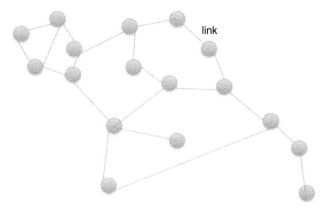

Figure 8.1 Link

We can see in both Figures 8.2 and 8.3 that the essential node within the organization, the one which connects two realities that otherwise would never communicate, is Cole. According to the organization chart, however, this node does not occupy a significant place in the formal structure and hierarchy of the organization. As a matter of fact, Cole is a connecting point between the production department and the rest of the organization. Some bad decisions can result from the lack of good knowledge of the relationships' semantics within an organization (not just of their grammar). The consequences of such decisions are not the ones expected since they do not directly involve the people who "make the difference" within the organization.

A deeper and clearer insight into the social network related to the organization might lead, instead, to the assignment of the right kind of tasks to the right people and increase, in this way, both the efficiency (the ability to do things "well") and the efficacy (the ability to do the "right" and necessary things). To keep to the topic of VBOs, the identification of the members of Group I and their placement in the right strategic positions (that are not necessarily hierarchically higher) might help the organization and foster a collaborative and productive environment within it by triggering the critical mass dynamics discussed in Chapter 6. But there is something more to say.

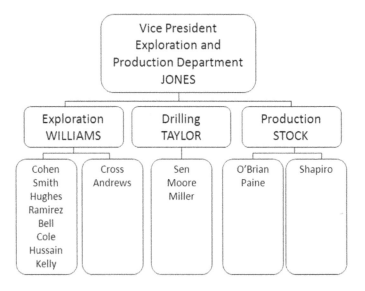

Figure 8.2 Organization chart

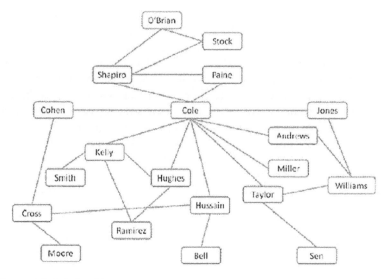

Figure 8.3 Relationship

In the example in question, the network analysis allows us to clearly see that the production department (the subgroup at the top of Figure 8.3) is isolated by the rest of the organization. As a matter of fact, a few months earlier this department was moved to another floor of the building removing, in this way, the opportunities for spontaneous interaction between its members and the other members of the organization. After examining the state of affairs, managers have decided to increase the number of formal meetings in order to compensate for the lack of other kinds of encounter.

A common mistake when the network morphology is not taken into consideration is to think that every member of the organization must be linked to every other member so that communications and information can reach everyone as soon as possible. This is, however, impossible and not even desirable, especially in complex organizations (in which there are a lot of nodes and links). As a matter of fact, there is evidence that inflexibility and great inefficiency might result from an uncontrolled increase in the links and communication within the organization. In the next section, we try to go deeper into the issue of networks by discussing their main typologies.

Types of network

There are at least three types of network.

The simplest form of network is the "star" one (see Figure 8.4). All the nodes within it are somehow connected to the central one but there are only a few links among them. In this type of network the clustering coefficient (the index which shows us the density of connections within a network) is equal to 0. There is only one person who is able to hold the nodes together while no communication and "peripheral" relationships between the single members exist.[2] Such is the case of organizations founded by a charismatic person, where relationships based on fidelity and loyalty are established between the members and the founder but not among the members of the organization or the community themselves. Even though a certain order and degree of efficiency exists in such organizations, as we have already discussed in previous chapters, they are very fragile and vulnerable. This is due to the fact that, once the founder is no longer present, it turns out that the members of the organization are not able to establish relationships between equals and from a state of order and efficiency the organization collapses into a stalemate and relational block.

The opposite to the "star" organization is the "random network" (see Figure 8.5), one where the links between different nodes are absolutely random and equally likely. In this type of network none of the nodes have special links with the other nodes and, consequently, a prominent place or leadership within the organization. An example of such a morphology of relationships are the groups of friends in which people spontaneously gather together for a short time and where the relational dynamics do not follow a particular formal or informal order (unless the group becomes stable: a situation in which a certain order emerges over time).

Finally, as we can see in Figure 8.6, a third type of network is the so called "small world" (or—in more technical terms—a *scale invariance network*).[3] In this kind of network it is possible to identify some special nodes, called hubs (just like at airports) that have a greater number of links in respect to the other nodes.

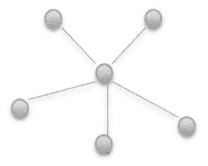

Figure 8.4 Star network

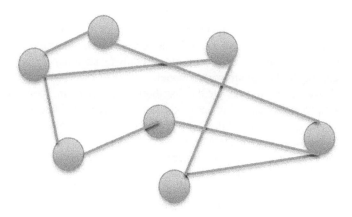

Figure 8.5 Random network

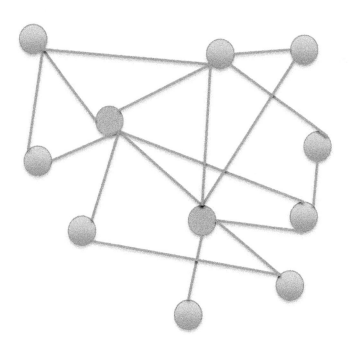

Figure 8.6 Small world network

The world of the internet is a good example of this small world network: its architecture is dominated by a few strongly connected nodes, such as Google, Yahoo, Amazon, etc. However, it seems that not only the web, but also social networks and networks in nature, or cellular, infrastructure and transport networks (such as airports and railway stations) can be described according to the "small world" model.

If we take as an example the distribution of airports in a country or continent, we notice some big ones—the hubs—which serve to connect the rest of the airports. It seems that the small world networks describe most faithfully the real trends in the world.

How are these three types of network reflected in the organizational structure? The *star* network describes a top-down, very hierarchical organization in which all links are in the hands of a single person. We have already mentioned that, as far as VBOs are concerned, this person is usually the founder who could actually be the source of some great ideals and projects but, at the same time, not foster the fraternity and friendship among the members of the organization. Therefore, such organizations turn out to be both strong and very fragile: strong while the founder is responsible for their management, they can collapse shortly after he leaves. Such a consequence is due exactly to the fact that all the links within the organization were related to this person.

The second type of network—the random one—is less common in nature: applied to an organization it would represent the kingdom of chaos. An organization in which there are links but random ones would be extremely difficult to manage. If some of its members default, others are influenced by these defections in a random way. The extent to which the organization is affected is proportional to the degree in which the nodes within it are interconnected, thus, to the clustering coefficient's value. The more the members are connected, the more a crisis would be indiscriminately spread within the entire organization.

What can we say about the *small world* networks? As already illustrated above, in these kind of networks there are some nodes—the hubs—more connected than the rest. Besides being the most common network among those spontaneously formed in nature or in society, the *small world* is also the most resistant network. Its presence within an organization means that there is more than one center of power and coordination—the so-called, connectors or the people who forge more bonds than others and whom it is easier to turn to when a problem needs to be solved.

Barabasi refers to the connectors or hubs as the nodes within a network who have high fitness:

> In a competitive environment each node has a certain fitness. Fitness is your ability to make friends relative to everybody else in your

neighborhood; a company's competence in luring and keeping consumers compared to other companies; an actor's aptitude for being liked and remembered relative to other aspiring actors; a Webpage's ability to bring us back on a daily basis relative to the billions of other pages competing for our attention. It is a quantitative measurement of a node's ability to stay in front of the competition.

(Barabasi 2005, p. 105)

What usually happens is that the new nodes, gradually joining the network, more often connect to the nodes who have higher fitness. It is as if the growth of the network was accompanied by the increase in the strength of its hubs. All of this contributes to the strength of the network itself: change or real innovation, when present, passes through the hubs and arrives at the entire network. In this way, they are spread across the organization.

What is the link between this brief examination of networks, VBOs and our analysis?

The theory of networks tells us that if during hard times the crisis affects the peripheral nodes, it will not spread to the entire organization. If the nodes affected are the hubs, instead, the effects of the crisis will be more devastating. In our analysis of VBOs until now we have seen that crises usually, in a particular way, when they concern the ideal quality of the organization, affect and drive towards the exit exactly the most motivated people who serve as a model for the others. As a matter of fact, if we use the language of networks, the most motivated people are the hubs of the VBO. And if the hubs are hit the network shortly collapses (especially when there are a few nodes whose clustering coefficient is high). Empirical evidence of these facts is provided by the numerous experiments carried out by Barabasi and other scholars who deal with the issue of social networks as well as by the historical experience of many communities and organizations.

This analysis strengthens some of the conclusions to which we had come by using our models. First, it confirms the thesis that it is extremely important to avoid the extreme consequences when the ideal quality is in crisis. This means avoiding the exit of the most motivated members who can be considered the hubs in the small world of the business network.

Second, the theory of hubs strengthens our previous conclusions concerning the fragility of those organizations that focus only or excessively on the intrinsically motivated individuals. A network centered on a single hub to which all other nodes are connected (a star network) would result from focusing only on these few members, or even the founder. If this single hub defaulted, the entire cooperative and ideal culture of the VBO would collapse. If there were, instead, more hubs within the organization, crises could be better managed and overcome. Here we find again the main message of our analysis that is coming to an end: that diversity and polycentrism support and strengthen the good reciprocity and cooperation and make organizations less fragile when faced with inevitable crises.

Notes

1 On these dynamics consult Cross-Parker (2004), pp. 7–8.
2 Cf. Barabasi (2005), pp. 51–52.
3 In a random network such as the one shown in Figure 8.5, almost all the nodes have the same number of links. Therefore, a random network has a typical scale represented by the average node—the one which has an average number of links. In the small world network, instead, there is no such idea as an average number of links: a link hierarchy can be noticed. It goes from the hubs (with a lot of links) which are not widespread, to the countless little nodes. Due to this feature such kinds of network are also called scale invariance networks.

9 Conclusion

Vulnerability as a human paradigm

Love is the most universal, the most formidable and the most mysterious of cosmic energies.

After groping search lasted for centuries, social institutions have been able to fight it and channel outside ...

On the social level, you pretend to ignore it in science, in business, in the assemblies, while, secretly, it is everywhere.

It seems to have come to despair to understand and capture this wild force, immense, ubiquitous, and increasingly untamed.

Then you let (and feel) it wind everywhere, under our civilization, asking, at most, to entertain and not to harm ...

Is it really possible that humanity continues to live and to grow without much questioning on what of truth and power it is squandering in its incredible ability to love?

(Pierre Teilhard de Chardin, *About Love*)

If economy, markets, companies and organizations are part of common life, then ideals have to find the right of citizenship even in the so-called "dismal science": Economy will always be a dismal science until the ideals and passions shall live in it, because only where gratuity lives, is it possible to meet the *joie de vivre*.

It is only by recognizing the right of citizenship to gratuity and to ideals in the social and economic life, that these environments, which are often heavy, can start to fly and make others fly.

For too long gratuity and ideals have been considered as "doing good," or as naïve behaviors that hurt themselves and those who perform them, because they allow the slyest to exploit them. In this book we have tried to show that, if properly understood, gratuity is a powerful force that can make the difference in organizations.

In the conclusion of this essay, we want to leave the final pages to further considerations on what really involves making space for gratuity and ideals in an organization.

One of the messages emerging more clearly from what has been argued could be summarized as follows: if we introduce the ideals, and with them the whole human world, within the life of our organizations and markets, relational dynamics develop and complicate. In fact, the "blessings" increase, but, at the same time, the "wounds" increase too.

The common life, sprinkled by ideals, is more worth living and promises an authentic human flourishing but, just because of its openness to whole humanity, when economy, organizations, and civil life meet with the ideals, we must take into account more and more relational sufferings and conflicts. However keep in mind that suffering is not only and always a bad thing, it is often only the other side of happiness, of the aristotelic *eudaimonia*.

In traditional medieval society, the possibility of life in community was closely bound to sacrifice and tragedy. The source of this vision is in Greek thought, predominantly in Aristotle's *Ethics*. Aristotle had grasped a paradox that is at the core of the entire West: a "good life," or a happy life, is at once civil and vulnerable. As noted in chapter IX of his *Nicomachean Ethics* (1169b) "the happy man needs friends"; this is why no one can be happy alone, and why it is impossible to achieve happiness in solitude and in flight from social life and encountering the other. But, if happiness requires social relationships, that is, requires friendship and reciprocity, and if friendship and reciprocity are free acts neither fully nor unilaterally controlled by the individual, then our happiness depends on the response of others, on how much they return our love, friendship and reciprocity. If, in other words, I need friends and reciprocity to be happy, then the happy life is ambivalent: the other is my joy and sorrow, my only chance for true happiness, but also he or she on whom my unhappiness depends. The "good life," the blessing, then depends on others, who however can hurt me.

Conversely, if to avoid this vulnerability and probable suffering I take refuge in solitude and contemplation apart from others (the great neoplatonic alternative), my life cannot fully flourish. This is why the Aristotelian tradition, beyond Aristotle himself, associates the happy life with tragedy. Regarding interpersonal relations, the contemporary thinker Martha Nussbaum states that "these components of the good life are going to be minimally self-sufficient. And they will be vulnerable in an especially deep and dangerous way" (1986, p. 344). In this sense, social life, the *communitas*, carries the mark of suffering within itself. The Jewish world reminds us, with several great symbols and myths contained primarily (but not solely) in Genesis, that the other is a blessing (because without him or her I cannot be happy), but also that he or she is the one who wounds me and whom I wound in turn (wounding and blessing always have a reciprocal nature).

Pre-modern and ancient thought understood the ambivalent nature of the good life: one cannot be happy without *communitas*, but precisely because of the need for relationship with the other and of his or her presence, the good life is intertwined in various ways with death. In this respect the foundational myths of ancient cities are emblematic. The first city (Enoch) in the Bible was founded by Cain, who killed his brother, and the founding of Rome is associated with the assassination of Remus by his brother Romulus. The idea of the common good in the pre-modern West was not associated with a sum of private interests; it entailed, so to speak, a subtraction: only by giving up and risking something of "one's own" (one's private goods) could one build something that is "ours" (the common good), which was common to all because it did not belong to anyone. We should, however, quickly note that the pre-modern worldview remained substantially holistic: the community is what is seen, not the individual. The Absolute absorbed everything; individuality did not emerge. There is One, not a manifold. In particular, ancient peoples did not consider the I–Thou relationship, or horizontal inter-subjectivity between equals. The ambivalence of life in community as lived, experienced, and known in flesh had not become a culture, either in the ancient world or in the pre-modern Christian West.

In fact, even the ingenious insights of Aristotle that we just mentioned about the need of friends for a good life should be read in a social and cultural context in which the friend is not really a Thou, but an alter ego, another self, as Aristotle states repeatedly: "A friend is another self" (*Nicomachean Ethics* 1170b).[1] Indeed, contemporary philosophers like Martha Nussbaum—whose paper, not by chance, opens this issue—are primarily the ones who load the reading of Aristotle's thought on social life with tragedy, but in the original thought of the great Greek philosopher the friend is chosen carefully and selectively precisely to minimize the possibility of negation, or the "not." One's friends are very few, because were there many the risk of injury, of betrayed reciprocity, would increase. In this sense, Aristotle's *philia* is selective and exclusive; the *philia* which is at the basis of the life of the polis is a *philia* among small numbers of equals (male, adult, and free, usually united by the same ethnicity, while those of mixed race, farmers, and merchants are excluded, as Aristotle carefully specifies in the first book of the Politics).

Friends do bring a certain diversity, but that of the Greeks is a "positive" diversity among similars; they seek a commonality among themselves into which the "not" that separates and wounds does not enter; there is no alterity. The polis for Aristotle, and the Greek world in general, was a community of equals, not of the dissimilar (as the Roman *civitas* tended to be), and the whole art of politics was avoiding the suffering due to the Thou-who-are-not-I. Only the polis is a place of relationship between equals, since all other groups that give rise to a polis (the village and the family) are unequal communities. Regarding the family, the basic unit of the state or the polis, Aristotle states that its "primary elements" are "master and servant, husband and wife, father and sons" (*Politics* 1232b), which are three types of radically unequal relationships. The polis must therefore be the place for these relationships among equals, the culmination—and here lies the paradox of this political vision—of a process of successive aggregations of unequal communities. That is why education is entrusted to the State and "is one and the same for all" (*Politics* 1337a).

In the ancient world, Greece included, interpersonal relationships were therefore always mediated by an Absolute, by a Third that avoided direct contact between people, symbolized by the community and its representatives. The community is seen as a single organism, to which supreme good all the parts are pre-ordained ("Neither must we suppose that any one of the citizens belongs to himself, for they all belong to the State," *Politics* 1337a).

I need not enter into deep relationship with you to be happy; my happiness sources from my relationship with the Absolute, with God. The fundamental pre-modern relational structure is thus triadic and unequal. The entire Middle Ages was thus a process of the slow emergence of individuality as a category, to the detriment of the *communitas*. This was a process that unfolded fairly peacefully through the Tuscan civil humanism of the first half of the fifteenth century, which then exploded in a rapid and irreversible proliferation with the Renaissance, the Reformation, the seventeenth century, and the Enlightenment.[2] It is in this cultural process that the rise of modern political economics must be situated.

One of the basic characteristics of modernity was the discovery of the other as a "Thou," a subjectivity that presents itself to me as different than me, but, at the same time, as a peer. The angel, the mysterious being who fought with Jacob, became the other. Once the Absolute had been eliminated from one's horizon, once the Sun had set, in this "twilight of the gods" modern humanity lowered its gaze, looked about, and became aware of the existence of the other, of an other-that-is-not-me. In the world of the One—as also in the Medieval Christian world—there was no room for two Absolutes: in the pre-modern world humanity recognized the transcendent Absolute and placed itself on a level of inferiority and submission to Him and his mediators.

The Absolute no longer exists in the modern world, and humanity finds itself before another like itself, but other than itself, in which every "I" represents the other "I" a "not," a non-being (if the other-who-is-not-me is, how can I exist?). Here, we have arrived at one crucial moment of this introduction to this special issue: the discovery of the other by modernity was the discovery of the negative, of the "not" that true otherness carries within itself. Modern humanity has seen primarily the wound, rather than the blessing, of the other. The reality of the self and of the other-that-is-not-I has not been associated with the positive and with happiness, but with the negative, with non-being, with "not." The enthusiasm for the discovery of my existence as a subject (and it was in fact enthusiasm, and legitimate enthusiasm, given the absolute importance of this discovery) was accompanied in modernity by the fear of the existence of the other. At the same instant in which a modern person says "I" he or she pronounces "you" fearfully, as if "you" were negating "I," and when constrained to say "you" he or she does everything possible not to recognize this "you" as an equal, nor is this "you" considered an indispensable source of his or her happiness. The discovery of the other did not become a means of mutual recognition, but opened a season—still fully developing—of searching for ways to avoid eye contact with the other.

Thomas Hobbes and Adam Smith represent two crucial moments in this epochal process in the social sciences. Hobbes with the Leviathan and Smith with the "Invisible Hand" of the market sought a replacement for the Absolute as the mediator of the I–Thou relationship. Faced with the "not" inherent in the discovery of the other, modern political and economic thought has not wanted to confront and traverse that negation, that wound; rather, as a matter of fact it returned to the inter-personal relational structure of pre-modernity, that of I/mediator/Thou, in which the mediator, instead of God, becomes the Leviathan or the Market—which, we should note, play the same role of impeding the passage through the risk that is the other, who comes alongside me as an equal.[3] There is thus a new metaphysics that takes the place of the pre-modern one (as the chosen metaphors themselves suggest: Leviathan is one monster in the book of Job in the Bible).

In Hobbes's politics and Smith's economics there is no direct intersubjectivity, but rather a mediated and anonymous relationality, for fear of the negative and the suffering that a personal "you" carries in him or herself. The contract—private for Smith, social for Hobbes—thus became the main instrument of this interaction, where the contract is above all that which is not a gift. But, without genuine and not mediated relationships happiness is not accomplished.

The modern social sciences were thus born from the invention of a new "thirdness" in new mediators, which however does not question the necessity of avoiding a dramatic interpersonal encounter. This new "third" is no longer the Third (God or *communitas*), nor a third that opens and universalizes the I–Thou relationship, that is, a third who is a "he" or "she" (in the fine sense of Emmanuel Lévinas), but a third that is immune from our relationship and which reciprocally "immunizes" us, and that guarantees (or promises) a free zone in which to meet each other without being wounded. In place of a "Thou," modernity preferred a "he," a neutral third that prevents our touching and hurting each other, a "someone" who, with Vladimir Jankélévitch (1970, p. 781), we could call "another," or, playing off the semantic richness of the French expression, *personne* (which can be understood as either "person," "someone" or "no one").

The liberal neo-contractarian theory is representative in this regard, especially in the version by John Rawls. Among its pre-theoretic terms the social contract requires that a "mutual disinterest" exist for one another (1971, pp. 128–129), since feelings, a sense of belonging, friendship and strong bonds are all dangerous, tending ever toward partiality and exclusivity. To be "just," a broad pluralistic and liberal society needs individuals without ties and passions. The differences between I and Thou are thus addressed by simply removing them; each protects him- or herself from these differences by increasingly sophisticated social and private contracts that do not require a dialogue, much less an interpersonal encounter, but precisely a mutual indifference.

In this sense contractual reciprocity in markets becomes a new form of reciprocity, a radical alternative to that based on a free and reciprocal gift; the gift brings us together since it requires that we find a common ground, which, by definition, belongs to neither of us, whereas the contract makes us immune from each other since what is mine is not yours, and vice-versa.[4] A common ground, especially when a place of relationships among equals, is also a place of conflict and death, a conflict and grief that modernity did not want to accept, renouncing as well—and this is the point—the life-giving fruit of that common ground. Modernity wanted to break the inevitability of this union, though without being able, and by paying a price that is proving too high.

There is a story in the Book of Genesis which is also an icon of the life of VBOs: *Jacob wrestling with the angel* (Genesis 32). After a long exile, also due to conflicts with his twin brother Esau (the ambivalent fraternity, which is always a wound!), Jacob returns to the land of his forefathers, bordered by the river Jabbok,[5] tumultuous tributary of the Jordan. Before coming back home, he has to cross the ford of the river during the night. Jacob is left alone, and a man wrestles with him. The man, in the course of the story, becomes a presence of God, Yahweh himself. The fight ends with Jacob a winner and wounded, with his hip socket wrenched. Jacob, however, asks that the man blesses him before leaving: having obtained the blessing, Jacob is renamed Israel, a name of a whole population, and for him "the sun was shining" (Genesis 33).

The message is clear: the O(o)ther is both a blessing and a wound, one is the way and the pre-condition of the other. When someone hurts me, he changes me deeply, he gives me a new name (in the Semitic world the name is the deeper reality, the vocation of the person).

The whole story, especially the modern one, is also an attempt to find new relationships that were only blessings, preserving us from the *wound of the other* (Bruni 2007, 2010). The solitary sadness of post-modernity, however, is also and above all an outcome of the immune project which separates one from each other to avoid the wounds of the relationship.

When the ideals *really* enter into the individual and collective life, in fact, something inevitable happens: you become vulnerable to another, because in these situations you can not immunize anymore behind the mediation or hierarchy of the price system (the two major immunizing tools of modern economics). We can not immunize from the diversity among human beings that is the primary source of relational sufferings when there arises a plan of true equality with each other.[6]

And when the wound of diversity is not accepted, the opening of the wound does not become fruitful, does not become a meeting place and an access point to another, but it becomes infected and festers in the thousands of diseases produced by the refused diversity, which are racism, discrimination, exclusion, etc.

Genesis does not give us clear guidance on what happened to the wound of Jacob after the fight, and it does not tell us clearly whether Jacob healed or if he continued to limp for life. There are only few allusions, some tracks and some rabbinic traditions that have developed on these clues contained in Genesis over millennia.

For example, in the same text of the fight, the sacred author wrote: "Therefore to this day the people of Israel do not eat the sciatic muscle that is on the hip socket" (Genesis 32: 33). And in the next chapter we find that "Jacob arrived safely at the city of Shechem" (Genesis 33: 18). To get "safely" to Shechem leads you to think that Jacob was healed from the wound, while the prohibition of eating the sciatic nerve seems to go in the opposite hermeneutic direction: eating is in fact a daily activity, and every day it should be noted that from the ford of the Jabbok it is no longer possible to separate the wound from the blessing, as also seen in some of the traditions of the midrashic literature.[7] The symbolic and vital power of the Bible is also present in these unwritten conclusions, in these ambivalences laden with symbols and truth.

We, not being experts in Scripture nor in Judaism, nor theologians, like to think that Jacob never healed that wound completely because when you stop "limping," you stop living.

The vulnerability, the exhibit of the other's wound (and mine to the other), is the *first condition of the human*. You stop living when you turn from fighting with each other, when you think you can live well without the exhibit of the wound, when you stop taking others' wounds, near and far, when you give up trying to heal and turn them into blessings.

We could express the same reality by saying that the two traditions (healing and limping) are not irreconcilable, because you really heal when you accept the condition of vulnerability, when we reconcile with our and others' deep wounds. It is, in fact, mutual awareness of vulnerability that creates the true reciprocity and cooperation among free men on a level of true equality.

After that fight, with God, with the other, but also with himself, Jacob is finally reconciled with his brother Esau after years of conflicts and deceptions: "Jacob looked up and saw Esau coming ... bowing to the ground seven times, until he reached his brother. Esau ran to meet him, embraced him, and flinging himself on his neck, kissed him and cried together" (Genesis 33: 1–4). Only after the fight and the wound in the thigh, Jacob is reconciled with his brother—nice they "cried together": how many reconciliations still end up with big tears together![8]—and only later Jacob is able to recognize him. A few lines later we read: "to come into your presence is for me like coming into the presence of God": now Jacob can see the image of God in his brother, respect him truly in his otherness, an otherness which is now a blessing, found over the wound. And only then Jacob can come back to the land of his forefathers to find deep roots of his own history and that of Israel.

There is no genuine care for the other without fighting.

We believe that when the protagonists of a VBO begin to not feel this wound and blessing dynamic, when its members stop fighting these good fights, this is a signal that the VBO has itself lost the *VB* (that is, values-based), remaining only a simple O, like many other Organizations. It is, in fact, the ability to see what is still lacking, unmet needs, denied rights, people not recognized or respected, which keeps a VBO alive, which feeds the ideal from which it originated, and makes it forever young.

For this "good" vulnerability (there is, of course, also a "bad" vulnerability that must be fought and eliminated if possible: that one of the children, the weak, the women in some regions of the world, the environment, animals, etc.), which in VBOs is particularly noted, and this for the reasons we have mentioned, it is necessary that in these organizations there are tools to properly understand, prevent and manage relational conflicts. This ability to care for and manage the conflicts must become a real art in VBOs, to grow and specialize in, to avoid first conflicts and deep wounds bringing the ideals of the VBO into deadly crisis, producing disappointment and cynicism in those who had genuinely believed they would be able to combine ideals and economic life.

Today there is an urgent need to invest in this art of managing relational conflicts in which our civilization is gravely deficient and immature: in the last two millennia we have invested significantly in technique and technology, and we have achieved outstanding results, but in our ability to care for and solve conflicts, in the art of difficult human relationships, we are still too similar to the fratricide Cain.

In a world that—despite the dreams of immunity—will force us more and more to meet the true diversity, the investment in this art is not less crucial than investments in renewable energies, because both the survival of our species and the quality of life—we will be able to create and store in the coming centuries—depend on them.

That the markets and our societies of the third millennium can be increasingly populated by ideals, gifts, gratuity, reciprocity, risky and vulnerable trust, happy passions, animated by actors more and more bearers of life all-round and increasingly experts in the art of human relationship caring: this is the hope we want to deliver as the final words of this book.

Notes

1 A certain philosophy of otherness, from Emmanuel Lévinas to Roberto Esposito, feels that it must overcome this Thou/alter-ego in an external "he/she" that makes relationality open and transcendent: "All the rhetoric of the excess of the other notwithstanding, in a one-on-one comparison, the other is conceivable only and ever in relation to the 'I'. The other cannot be but non-self, its reverse and its shadow" (Roberto Esposito 2007, p. 129).

2 In Bruni (2006), there is a reconstruction of this historical evolution that led to the rise of modern individualist economics; see this work for further study.

3 There would be much to say regarding the Protestant culture in which both Hobbes and Smith worked; the rejection of mediators in fact created other mediators that, in the long run, are emerging as tyrants no less fierce than those of pre-modern times.

4 Roberto Esposito in fact points out that the most radical contradiction is not the one between community and society (as in classic social thought) but between *communitas* and *immunitas* (immunity).

5 In Hebrew Jabbok is a sort of anagram of the name of Jacob (Yacob), to emphasize, perhaps, that the battle of Jacob is also a fight with himself, in search of his identity and vocation, which comes out as Israel.

6 Much of the relational and spiritual growth of a person is to understand that there are wounds that others will procure which are not the result of their wickedness, nor of our own, but of diversity.

7 "The abstention from consumption of the sciatic nerve is the only law of the kashrut to have a memory function. Of course if we exclude the laws of Passover, which have indeed a similar function but are linked to the festival and not to the kashrut itself. The sciatic nerve is called in the Torah gid hanasheh, bond of forgetfulness. This name refers, in fact, to the very notion of memory, and the lack thereof. This singular prohibition is probably directed to remember ... that Jacob reaches his fullness through the wound, through the limp" (http://lnx. levchadash.info).

8 Actually, we have not enough data to know if Esau really forgave Jacob: in the rabbinic literature there is a certain ambivalence (even because Esau, ancestor of the Edomites, is also the symbol of the nations around Israel: that hug has always been loaded with complex historical and political meanings), but we also like the ambivalence because the hug with the other has a value in itself even if it lasts only the time to embrace, and if, for our frailties, peace—reconciliation can not last. Not all the relationships can be enlivened completely and forever, and not all the wounds can become solid blessings: but this does not detract from the infinite value of a reconciliation hug.

Appendix 1
Cooperation and diversity[1]

In this appendix we present a different, and more analytical, version of the three types of model that are at the center of our theory of VBOs. In particular, here the three types can be interpreted as forms of cooperation analogies—although they are not identical to our three groups in the analysis of the previous chapters. In this Appendix there are four kinds of behaviours (strategies), and the "brave" and the "cautious" strategies can be considered a specification of what we call in this book the Group III—being all conditional cooperators, intermediate forms between the extreme "always" and "never" cooperate.

The conclusion of the model of the Appendix confirms the crucial role of the "unconditional cooperator" (i.e. Group I), but adds also something more, namely the importance that the unconditional agents (or actions) are not too many, otherwise the excessive presence of unconditional reciprocity within a organization will, unintentionally, foster non-reciprocity. In conclusion, some more general consideration on this result will be supplied and discussed.

Civil life is essentially cooperation. Neoclassical economics offers mostly a parsimonious view of cooperation based merely on individual self-interests and instrumental rationality. In such a vision of cooperation, an agent will never cooperate in a one-shot game of Prisoner's Dilemma. If instead the game is repeated, the traditional theory justifies the cooperation by evoking self-interest and/or enforcement (Binmore 2005, 2006). In reaction to this parsimonious view of cooperation, recent years have seen development of a body of literature (mainly experimental), the so-called "social preferences" theories, which instead seek to explain why it may even be rational to play "cooperatively" in a one-shot non-cooperative game (i.e. the "ultimatum" or "trust" game). The explanation, of which there are several variants, is a redefinition of the utility function of the agents, by introducing non-material payoffs associated to norms such as inequality aversion or reciprocity. In this way it is possible to explain the emergence of cooperative behaviour in contexts where the standard theory would exclude it. This is the explanation of cooperation advanced by behavioural economists (see Gintis 2004 and

Bowles and Gintis 2004), who base their analyses of cooperation on the theory of strong reciprocity (Fehr and Gächter 2000). By "strong reciprocity" they mean a social norm that rewards those who behave in a kind way and punishes those who behave in an unkind way. This theory explains the emergence of cooperation on the basis of a form of altruism, which does not require the repetition of the game. In this paper we adopt a different approach for explaining the emergence of cooperation in an evolutionary scenario. We propose a pluralistic and multidimensional view of cooperation and consequently examine aspects hitherto not suffciently explored by economic and social theory. In particular, the intuition inspiring this paper is the multidimensional nature of cooperation: civil society flourishes if and when different forms of reciprocity are seen as complementary rather than rival or substitutes for one another. In this sense, we shall show that diversity fosters cooperation, a result well known in biology. Specifically, we claim to show on the one hand that, in certain settings, less "altruistic," conditional forms of cooperation may combine with unconditional ones generating a cooperative environment. On the other hand, we'll demonstrate that too many unconditional actions will in the end promote non-cooperation. The combination of these two results embodies the main contribution of this paper. We accordingly construct models of evolutionary game theory, which will enable us to analyse diverse patterns of cooperation, not all of them based on self-interest, but all of them important for understanding the dynamics of civil life. We shall base our analysis on the dynamic Prisoner's Dilemma (PD) game, because it lends itself well to the modeling of "diffcult" cooperation, the kind that occurs in situations where there is no enforcement and where there is always an incentive for non-cooperation. We believe that these situations are frequent and relevant—although in civil society individuals play many games, not only the PD—and that they are important in the real dynamics of cooperation in civil life.

In section 2 we introduce our model. In section 3 we analyse the evolution of cooperation in a context of repeated games. In section 4 we concentrate on analysis of situations in which four strategies interact, also making some simulations. The paper concludes with a brief discussion of the results of our analysis.

The repeated dynamic game

The pay-off matrix of the game is the following.[2]

	C	D
C	$\beta - \gamma$	$-\gamma$
D	B	0

It can be easily shown that both players will choose not to cooperate or defect (D) in a one-shot game, and that the outcome (0, 0) will be a Nash equilibrium.[3] In this kind of non-iterated game cooperation cannot arise unless errors are committed or the players behave irrationally.

The structure of our model is as follows. Time is continuous. We suppose that there is a continuum of agents belonging to a particular population, and that they must choose one of the J pure strategies $\{1, \dots, J\}$ whenever they interact with other subjects in the same population. The subjects are distributed among I sub-populations $\{1, \dots, I\}$, which are assigned exogenously in the sense that existing sub-populations may disappear but new ones cannot be created.

The model's dynamic is described by standard "replication" equations. The replication dynamic is widely used in evolutionary models, which assume that the most profitable strategies proliferate in the population at the expense of others. Heckathorn (1996) describes this dynamic well:

> Based on the resulting payoffs, the actors with the most successful strategies proliferate at the expense of the less successful. This process is then repeated, generation after generation, until the system either approaches stable equilibrium or cyclical variation.
>
> (p. 261)

This dynamic is usually employed in biology to study the evolution of species on the basis of the relative *fitness*. However, in social sciences there is a different interpretation of such a selection process: it involves learning by observing and imitating the behaviour of others. In what follows, we adopt neither the biological analogy nor the memetic one (i.e. the extension of gene-based biological evolution to meme-based social evolution). Instead, we use the concept of "expected utility" as an indicator of the success (not necessarily material) of a strategy: a success which, over time, is imitated by less successful strategies (those with less expected utility). The dynamic of the model can be represented by the replication equations:

$$\dot{p}_i = p_i(Y_i - Y) \qquad i = 1, \dots N \tag{1}$$

where p denotes the proportion of subjects for each subpopulation, Y the average payoff, and Y_i the average payoff for a subject belonging to the subpopulation i.

The dynamic is defined on the invariant simplex:

$$\Delta = \left\{ p \notin \Re^N, \sum_{i=1}^{N} p_i = 1, p_i \geq 0 \right\}$$

We shall use this analytical structure to analyse the evolutionary process that arises in a situation where there are two pure strategies, C and D, and first two, then three, and finally four sub-populations.

We are well aware that if the game is repeated, the possible strategies are infinite. We consequently restrict our analysis to four strategies. Two of them are called, following Sugden (2004), B (= Brave) and C (= Cautious).

The strategies considered are therefore the following:

1   N: never cooperate. N is a highly important strategy because analysis of cooperation dynamics becomes non-banal precisely when non-cooperation scenarios are possible.

2   G: always cooperate.

3   C: cooperate with a player who cooperated in the previous round; do not cooperate with a player who did not cooperate in the previous round, and *begin by not cooperating*. If these cautious types are to cooperate, they must have obtained cooperation in the previous round. When Cs encounter other Cs or Ns, they never cooperate. An immediate consequence ensues: in a world with only Cs and Ns, cooperation will never be possible, and it will not be possible to distinguish Cs from Ns because they behave in exactly the same way.

4   B: this strategy has the same structure as C, the only difference being that B begins by cooperating. In fact B stands for "Brave." Bs are players who begin by cooperating (and therefore risk being "exploited" by Ns or Cs in the first round). But if in the second round they do not receive cooperation, they will not cooperate.

If we use p_n, p_b, p_g and p_c to denote the probabilities of encountering, respectively, an N, B, G or C type, the expected utilities in a world with these four possible strategies are:

$$U_n = p_n(0) + p_b\beta + p_g\frac{\beta}{1-\pi} + p_c(0) \qquad [2]$$

An N type will never cooperate with other N types, and with C types who begin by not cooperating and do not cooperate if the other player did not cooperate in the first round, whence $p_n(0)$, $p_c(0)$. If the N type encounters a B type, s/he will obtain β in the first round because B began with an act of cooperation, but the subsequent payoffs will be equal to 0 because B will stop cooperating from the second round onwards. Finally, if N encounters a G, s/he will obtain β in every round[4] because G will always cooperate.

$$U_b = p_n(-\gamma) + p_b\frac{(\beta-\gamma)}{1-\pi} + p_g\frac{(\beta-\gamma)}{1-\pi} + p_c(-\gamma + \beta\pi) \qquad [3]$$

The B type begins with an act of cooperation and continues to cooperate if the adversary in the first round has responded by cooperating. Cooperation is assured with other B types and with G types, but not with N types, or even with C types.[5]

$$U_g = p_n \frac{-\gamma}{1-\pi} + p_b \frac{(\beta-\gamma)}{1-\pi} + p_g \frac{(\beta-\gamma)}{1-\pi} + p_c \left(\frac{\beta-\gamma}{1-\pi} - \beta \right) \qquad [4]$$

A G type will therefore always cooperate with Bs and with Gs, and with Cs from the second round onwards, while Gs will let themselves be "exploited" by Ns.

$$U_c = p_n(0) + p_b(\beta - \gamma\pi) + p_g \left(\frac{\beta-\gamma}{1-\pi} + \gamma \right) + p_c(0) \qquad [5]$$

Finally, a C type will not cooperate with Ns and Cs, and s/he will cooperate with Gs from the second round onwards. With Bs, C types will receive β in the first round, given that Bs begins with an act of cooperation, and $(-\gamma)$ in the second round. From the third round onwards Cs will obtain 0.

The evolutionary analysis

In order to analyse the evolution in dynamic terms, we consider three strategies at a time (so that we can use simplexes).

After the first game, it is likely that the proportion of players adopting the winning strategy will increase in future pairings: i.e., the winning strategy will be imitated by others. This will be the basis for *both* our *repeated and evolutionary* analysis.

It will be assumed in the analysis that $\pi > \dfrac{\gamma}{\beta}$ [6]

First case: N, C, G

We begin the analysis with B types omitted.

The replication dynamic can be represented in Figure A.1. When strategies N, C and G are present, the outcome may be one of the multiple fixed points along the line N–C, which signifies *non-cooperation*. If only strategies G and C are present, the outcome may be a unique combination of C and G that depends on the position of the point (in this case a saddle point), g, i.e.:

$$g \equiv \left(0, \frac{\gamma(1-\pi)}{(\beta-\gamma)\pi}, \frac{\beta\pi-\gamma}{(\beta-\gamma)\pi} \right)$$

Other conditions remaining equal, if $\gamma \to 1$—so that the likelihood of continuing with the same person initially encountered is very high—the point shifts towards vertex G.

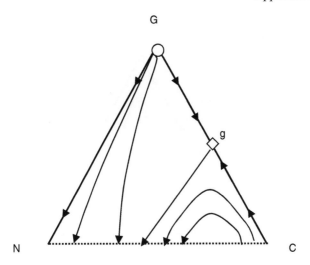

Figure A.1 N, C, G

This result strikes us as important: only G types are able somehow to activate Cs, who without Gs would always be confined to a world of non-cooperation.

The following proposition therefore holds:

Proposition 1. In a world in which the types or strategies N, G, C are present, the replication dynamic has two different outcomes: a combination of C and G (fixed point g) only if p_n is equal to 0, or a combination along the line of fixed points N, C (and consequently non-cooperation).

Without the presence of B types—who always begin with an act of cooperation—it is unlikely that virtuous cooperation mechanisms will be triggered.

Second case: N, B, C

Another interesting case is that in which G types are absent. Here too, non-cooperation is a probable equilibrium. The other equilibrium is the one where only B strategies survive. In a three-strategy world in which only Ns, Cs and Bs are present, in fact, Ns and Cs will never cooperate, and moreover the Ns will have no Gs to exploit. Instead, the Bs will cooperate only and exclusively with each other, obtaining a greater payoff—if the game lasts for a long time—than that received by the Ns and the Cs.

Here too, as shown by Figure A.2, the possible long-period equilibrium depends on the coordinates of the fixed point *f*.

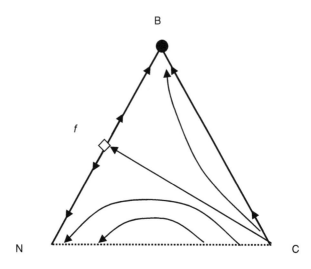

Figure A.2 N, B, C

All the points of departure in the simplex lying below the trajectory from C to *f* will evolve towards a non-cooperative equilibrium if N and C are present.

Proposition 2. In a world in which the types or strategies N, C, B are present, the replication dynamic has two different outcomes: the survival of B strategies alone, or a combination along the line of fixed points N, C (and consequently non-cooperation).

The coordinates of point *f* are now:

$$f \equiv \left(\frac{\beta\pi - \gamma}{(\beta - \gamma)\pi} \quad 0 \quad \frac{\gamma(1 - \pi)}{(\beta - \gamma)\pi} \right)$$

It is evident that if the point tends to shift towards the N vertex, so that the greater the probability of the game continuing, the more likely it becomes that Bs will prevail and that the cooperative outcome will occur. In a world without G types, Cs do not begin to cooperate. We may say that the sacrifice of the Gs somehow restores cooperation potential to Cs, for without their presence the only possible form of cooperation is that between B types. To be noted is that B types begin with an act of cooperation. In their absence, a non-cooperative equilibrium would arise.

Third case: N, B, G

The simplex relative to this third and final case shows that, depending on the point of departure and the position of fixed point *f* on the N–B side, there will be a different final equilibrium, which may be a combination of G and B, or a world consisting only of Ns (Figure A.3). Matters are different when the three types instead coexist in the population at time 1 (when the dynamic begins). In this case, non-reciprocity, i.e. an equilibrium consisting of only N types, may prevail.

Proposition 3. In a world in which the strategies N, B, G are present, two equilibria are possible: the survival of only N types and a coexistence of B types and G types along the line of fixed points on the B–G side. Which of the two equilibria will come about depends on the position of the fixed point f along the N–B side.

As the simplex is constructed here, considering that the position of N in terms of fraction of the population is (1,0,0) and the position of B is (0,1,0), the fixed point *f* has the following coordinates:

$$f \equiv \left(\frac{\beta\pi - \gamma}{(\beta - \gamma)\pi}, \; \frac{\gamma(1 - \pi)}{(\beta - \gamma)\pi}, \; 0 \right)$$

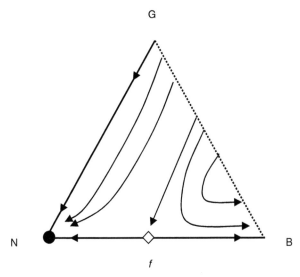

Figure A.3 N, B, G

The position of point f therefore depends on β and γ, and on the value of π. In particular, for $\pi \to \dfrac{\gamma}{\beta}$ point f will approach B. If instead $\gamma \to 1$, point f will shift towards N. With a small value of π, ceteris paribus, the likelihood that only N types will prevail is very high; instead, with a very high π, it very likely that the final equilibrium will be the one in which B types and G types coexist.

For every intermediate value between the two extremes, the final equilibrium will depend on the point of departure: if this is a point to the left of the trajectory leading from side B–G to point f, then the tendency is an equilibrium of only Ns; vice versa, if the point of departure is to the right of the trajectory, the outcome will be a coexistence of Bs and Gs. Note that points to the left are characterized, amongst other things, by a lower percentage of Bs than of Gs. It is therefore important that B types be relatively more than Gs and Ns for the B–G equilibrium to come about. In short, evident here is the delicate role of G strategies: if there are too many of them, they foster the emergence of N types over Bs. Metaphors aside, in a population where non-cooperation is possible, if there are too many unconditional acts, not only are they likely to become extinct, but they will also extinguish the possibility of cooperation, for an equilibrium consisting of non-generalized cooperation.

At the same time, the coordinates of point f also depend on β and γ. The value of γ is the one which most clearly tells us what the social rewards structure is. A high γ denotes a culture which penalizes reciprocity, while a high $(\beta\text{-}\gamma)$ denotes a culture which rewards it. In fact, if the first coordinate is high, point f tends to N (the same happens if the second coordinate is low), while if it is low f tends to B.

This is because the coordinate of N is directly proportional to β: while both coordinates depend on $(\beta\text{-}\gamma)$, the sign of γ is negative in the coordinate of N and positive in the coordinate of B. This tells us that the more a society, ceteris paribus, makes reciprocity of G and B type costly, the more likely the prevalence of non-cooperation becomes.

In a four-dimensional world

Thus far we have compared three strategies at a time, and we have analysed their dynamic evolution. The question now is what changes if the four strategies N, B, G, C interact simultaneously.

In the four-strategies case, the replication dynamic can be depicted by a three-dimensional simplex:

$$\Delta = \left\{ p \in \mathfrak{R}^4 : p \geq 0 \ e \ p_n + p_b + p_g + p_c = 1 \right\}$$

In this case matrix A becomes:

$$A = \begin{pmatrix} 0 & \beta & \dfrac{\beta}{1-\pi} & 0 \\[2ex] -\gamma & \dfrac{\beta-\gamma}{1-\pi} & \dfrac{\beta-\gamma}{1-\pi} & \beta\pi-\gamma \\[2ex] \dfrac{-\gamma}{1-\pi} & \dfrac{\beta-\gamma}{1-\pi} & \dfrac{\beta-\gamma}{1-\pi} & \dfrac{\beta\pi-\gamma}{1-\pi} \\[2ex] 0 & \beta-\pi\gamma & \dfrac{\beta-\pi\gamma}{1-\pi} & 0 \end{pmatrix} \qquad [7]$$

The vector ${}^t\mathbf{p} \equiv (p_m, p_b, p_w, p_c)$, so that the system of equations becomes:

$$\dot{p}_n = p_n \left[(Ap)_1 - {}^t p \times Ap) \right]$$
$$\dot{p}_b = p_b \left[(Ap)_2 - {}^t p \times Ap) \right]$$
$$\dot{p}_g = p_g \left[(Ap)_3 - {}^t p \times Ap) \right]$$
$$\dot{p}_c = p_c \left[(Ap)_4 - {}^t p \times Ap) \right] \qquad [8]$$

Given that analysis of the system of differential equations [8] would be highly complex, here we only report the frontier conditions (those in which at least one strategy is extinct). Following the examples of Hirshleifer and Martinez Coll (1991), and of Antoci, Sacco and Zarri (2004), we may represent the surface (or frontier) of Δ on the plane. The simplex Δ can be imagined as having a triangular base N, C, B, and G as its upper vertex (if the simplex in Figure A.4 were drawn three-dimensionally, the three vertices G would become a single upper vertex).

Figure A.4 shows that there are four possible equilibrium combinations:

- a combination of G and B, i.e. cooperation;
- a combination of N and C, i.e. non-cooperation;
- the extinction of all the strategies except N;
- the extinction of all the strategies except B.

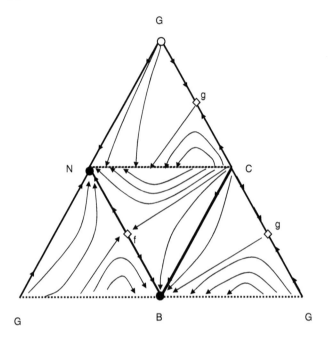

Figure A.4 Four dimensions

Some simulations

Which of these equilibria are more likely depends on the initial conditions.
To furnish a clearer idea of the dynamic, we now report some simulations.
They have been obtained by setting various initial conditions for the system.
We assigned the following values to the parameters:

$$\beta = 2, \gamma = 1, \pi = 4/5$$

The first graph shows the evolution over time of the strategies when the
initial conditions state: $p_n = p_b = p_g = p_c = 0.25$.

In this case the final equilibrium is of the B–G type where the proportion of G is very small. What happens if we change the initial conditions?
Figure A.5 illustrates a situation where the initial proportions are $p_n = 0.25$,
$p_b = 0.25$, $p_g = 0.1$, $p_c = 0.4$. We have left the proportions of B and G unal-
tered, but we have increased Cs with respect to Gs.

Interestingly, a greater proportion of Cs, although it does not improve
their chances of 'survival', helps the development of Gs, which in this case

remain constant over time. We saw previously that only G types are able to activate Cs; we may now state that Cs are essential for the survival of Gs. The importance of the role performed by Cs (which in the three-strategy world seemed almost irrelevant) also emerges from Figure A.6, which has been constructed with the following initial proportions: $p_n = 0.4, p_b = 0.3, p_g = 0.1, p_c = 0.2$. In this case the Ns are initially in a greater proportion than Bs, and there are more Cs than Gs.

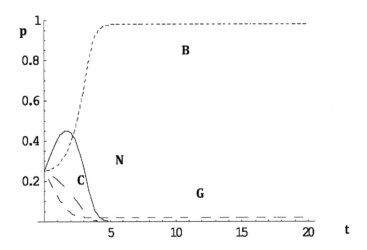

Figure A.5 Simulation with same initial proportion

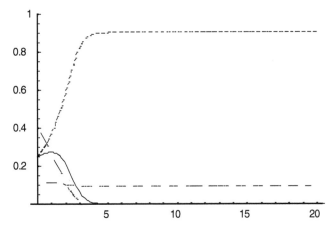

Figure A.6 Simulation with a greater proportion of Cs

Hence, cooperation may prevail even if there are initially more Ns than Bs, provided that there is a sufficient number of Cs.

Conclusions

Now we may draw some conclusions, that can be summarised as follows:

(a) *The "crucial" role of G types.* We have seen at various points in our analysis that G types should not be too numerous, because if they are they compromise themselves and also the survival, for example, of Bs. In populations where non-cooperation is possible (which is the case of all real ones), unconditional acts are essential, but when too numerous, they become counter-productive.

(b) G types perform a vital role, for only they can activate the cooperation of Cs. Without the presence of G types, Cs would never experience cooperation and therefore would never respond with an act of cooperation. G types are consequently valuable, but they should be protected. The success of numerous forms of cooperation—from firms to families—depends also, and sometimes above all, on the presence of a small number of unconditional reciprocators able to activate people who would never be so activated if they only interacted with conditional cooperators.

(c) *Alliances: C types.* These are "activated" by Gs, but at the same time their presence is highly beneficial to Gs because it increases their expected utility. Gs, in fact, cooperate with Bs and with Cs, but they are exploited by Ns. In a four-strategy world, Cs protect the Gs against extinction.

Cooperation is therefore favoured by heterogeneity.

From a mathematical point of view, it might be objected that G types are not necessary. The onset of cooperation would only require slightly more sophisticated Bs. But this was not the purpose (i.e. to study which strategies favour cooperation) for which the model was conceived. Our analysis started from the assumption that behaviours like G exist in civil society. (And who could deny the presence in the real world of unconditional actions? Even Binmore (2006) with his orthodoxy and anthropological parsimony admits their existence.) Our model has sought to analyze the conditions under which unconditional actions can not only survive but also perform a virtuous civil role.

Appendix 2
Mathematical appendix

Proof of proposition 1
The expected utilities are:

$$U_n = p_n(0) + p_c(0) + p_g \frac{\beta}{1-\pi}$$

$$U_c = p_n(0) + p_c(0) + p_g \frac{\beta - \gamma\pi}{1-\pi}$$

$$U_n = p_n\left(\frac{-\gamma}{1-\pi}\right) + p_c\left(\frac{\beta\pi - \gamma}{1-\pi}\right) + p_g \frac{\beta - \gamma}{1-\pi}$$

The matrix of payoffs is:

$$A = \begin{pmatrix} 0 & 0 & \dfrac{\beta}{1-\pi} \\[2mm] 0 & 0 & \dfrac{\beta - \pi\gamma}{1-\pi} \\[2mm] \dfrac{-\gamma}{1-\pi} & \dfrac{\beta\pi - \gamma}{1-\pi} & \dfrac{\beta - \gamma}{1-\pi} \end{pmatrix}$$

Adding a constant to each column of A does not change the dynamics, so we subtract the first row:

$$A = \begin{pmatrix} 0 & 0 & 0 \\[2mm] 0 & 0 & \dfrac{-\pi\gamma}{1-\pi} \\[2mm] \dfrac{-\gamma}{1-\pi} & \dfrac{\beta\pi - \gamma}{1-\pi} & \dfrac{-\gamma}{1-\pi} \end{pmatrix}$$

We know that $\beta > \gamma > 0$.

Following Bomze (1983), proposition 1 (page 210):

1   the eigenvalue of the corner N in direction N–C is equal to 0

2   the eigenvalue of the corner N in direction N–G is proportional to $\dfrac{-\gamma}{1-\pi}$, and then is negative

3   the eigenvalue of the corner C in direction C–N is equal to 0

4   the eigenvalue of the corner C in direction C–G is proportional to $\dfrac{\beta\pi-\gamma}{1-\pi}$, and then is positive (we have supposed that $\pi > \dfrac{\gamma}{\beta}$)

5   the eigenvalue of the corner G in direction G–C is proportional to $\dfrac{\gamma-\pi\gamma}{1-\pi}$, and then is positive

6   the eigenvalue of the corner G in direction G–N is proportional to $\dfrac{\gamma}{1-\pi}$, and then is positive.

Following proposition 2 (page 210) we know that N–C is pointwise fixed.

Proposition 5 (page 211) tells us that there exists a fixed point g (saddle point) on the side G–C, in fact the quantity $(e-b)(f-c)$ is negative, and the eigenvalues associated to the fixed point are proportional to:

1   $-\dfrac{(e-b)(c-f)}{e-b+c-f}$, that means $\dfrac{-\left(\dfrac{\beta\pi-\gamma}{1-\pi}\right)\left(\dfrac{\gamma-\pi\gamma}{1-\pi}\right)}{\dfrac{\beta\pi-\pi\gamma}{1-\pi}}$ this quantity is negative;

2   $\dfrac{bf-ce}{e-b+c-f}$, that is positive.

Proof of proposition 2

Expected utilities:

$$U_n = p_n(0) + p_c(0) + p_b(\beta)$$
$$U_c = p_n(0) + p_c(0) + p_b(\beta - \gamma\pi)$$
$$U_b = p_n(-\gamma) + p_c(\beta\pi - \gamma) + p_b\left(\dfrac{\beta-\gamma}{1-\pi}\right)$$

Matrices:

$$\begin{pmatrix} 0 & 0 & \beta \\ 0 & 0 & \beta - \gamma\pi \\ -\gamma & \beta\pi - \gamma & \dfrac{\beta - \gamma}{1 - \pi} \end{pmatrix} \text{ and } \begin{pmatrix} 0 & 0 & 0 \\ 0 & 0 & -\gamma\pi \\ -\gamma & \beta\pi - \gamma & \dfrac{\beta\pi - \gamma}{1 - \pi} \end{pmatrix}$$

and:

1   the eigenvalue of the corner N in direction N–C is equal to 0

2   the eigenvalue of the corner N in direction N–B is proportional to $-\gamma$, and then is negative

3   the eigenvalue of the corner C in direction C–N is equal to 0

4   the eigenvalue of the corner C in direction C–G is proportional to $\beta\pi - \gamma$, and then is positive

5   the eigenvalue of the corner B in direction B–C is proportional to $\dfrac{-\beta\pi + \gamma - \pi\gamma + \pi^2\gamma}{1 - \pi}$, and then is negative

6   the eigenvalue of the corner B in direction B–N is proportional to $\dfrac{\gamma - \beta\pi}{1 - \pi}$, and then is negative.

Following proposition 2 (page 210) we may say:

- the side N–C is pointwise fixed
- on the side N–B there exists a unique fixed point f; the eigenvalues of f are positively proportional to:
  - γ (positive)
  - $\dfrac{0 - (-\gamma\pi)(-\gamma)}{\dfrac{\beta\pi - \gamma}{1 - \pi}}$ (negative).

The fixed point has coordinates (Bomze 1983, page 204):

$$p_n = \frac{1}{1 + \dfrac{\gamma}{\dfrac{\beta\pi - \gamma}{1 - \pi}}} = \frac{\beta\pi - \gamma}{(\beta - \gamma)\pi}$$

$$p_c = 0$$

$$p_b = \frac{\gamma(1 - \pi)}{(\beta - \gamma)\pi}$$

We know that fixed points on the side C–B do not exist (proposition 5) and that internal fixed points do not exist (proposition 6).

Proof of proposition 3

Expected utilities:

$$U_n = p_n(0) + p_b\beta + p_g \frac{\beta}{1-\pi}$$

$$U_b = p_n(-\gamma) + p_b \frac{\beta-\gamma}{1-\pi} + p_g \frac{\beta-\gamma}{1-\pi}$$

$$U_g = p_n\left(\frac{-\gamma}{1-\pi}\right) + p_b \frac{\beta-\gamma}{1-\pi} + p_g \frac{\beta-\gamma}{1-\pi}$$

Matrices:

$$\begin{pmatrix} 0 & \beta & \dfrac{\beta}{1-\pi} \\[2ex] -\gamma & \dfrac{\beta-\gamma}{1-\pi} & \dfrac{\beta-\gamma}{1-\pi} \\[2ex] \dfrac{-\gamma}{1-\pi} & \dfrac{\beta-\gamma}{1-\pi} & \dfrac{\beta-\gamma}{1-\pi} \end{pmatrix} \text{ and } \begin{pmatrix} 0 & 0 & 0 \\[2ex] -\gamma & \dfrac{\beta\pi-\gamma}{1-\pi} & \dfrac{-\gamma}{1-\pi} \\[2ex] \dfrac{-\gamma}{1-\pi} & \dfrac{\beta\pi-\gamma}{1-\pi} & \dfrac{-\gamma}{1-\pi} \end{pmatrix}$$

1   the eigenvalue of the corner N in direction N–B is proportional to $-\gamma$, and then is negative

2   the eigenvalue of the corner N in direction N–G is proportional to $\dfrac{-\gamma}{1-\pi}$, and then is negative

3   the eigenvalue of the corner B in direction B–N is proportional to $-\dfrac{\beta\pi-\gamma}{1-\pi}$, and then is negative

4   the eigenvalue of the corner B in direction B–G is equal to 0

5   the eigenvalue of the corner G in direction G–B is equal to 0

6   the eigenvalue of the corner G in direction G–N is equal to $\dfrac{\gamma}{1-\pi}$, and then is positive.

We know that there exists a fixed point on the side N–B (proposition 2), and that the eigenvalues of the fixed point are positively proportional to γ, then positive

$$\frac{\left(\dfrac{\beta\pi-\gamma}{1-\pi}\right)\left(\dfrac{-\gamma}{1-\pi}\right)-(-\gamma)\left(\dfrac{\beta\pi-\gamma}{1-\pi}\right)}{\dfrac{\beta\pi-\gamma}{1-\pi}},$$

that becomes $\dfrac{-\gamma\pi}{1-\pi}$, and then is negative.

The fixed point has coordinates (Bomze 1983: 204):

$$p_m = \frac{1}{1+\dfrac{\gamma}{\dfrac{\beta\pi-\gamma}{1-\pi}}} = \frac{\beta\pi-\gamma}{(\beta-\gamma)\pi}$$

$$p_b = \frac{\gamma(1-\pi)}{(\beta-\gamma)\pi}$$

$$p_w = 0$$

We also know that the side B–G is pointwise fixed.

Notes

1 An earlier and partially different version of this appendix was first published in Bruni and Smerilli (2012).
2 The table represents a particular case which simplifies the analysis without compromising the results. As well known, for a game to be a Prisoner's Dilemma, the payoff order must be $\beta > \gamma > 0$.
3 This equilibrium represents a dilemma because the outcome of the game is non-cooperation when each player individually prefers mutual cooperation. It is well known that the outcome of the game depends essentially on two assumptions concerning rationality (individualism and instrumentality) and on an assumption concerning the type of interaction (anonymous). On this see Bruni (2006) and Bruni and Smerilli (2004).
4 Hence the expected utility associated to this interaction is
   $\beta + \beta\pi + \beta\pi^2 + \dots$ and then when n tends to infinite $\beta_1 - \pi$
5 The payoff depends on the fact that B cooperates the first time and C responds by not cooperating; B will therefore have $(-\gamma)$, but C will cooperate in the second round, because B has cooperated in the first. From the third round onwards the payoff will be 0.
6 We imagine, in fact, that two players agree to cooperate in each round. If they abide by the agreement, the expected utility of each player is $\beta - \gamma 1 - \pi$. However, if one of the players breaks the agreement, the other will no longer cooperate. Thus a player who breaks the agreement in the first round will receive β, but from the second round onwards s/he will always receive 0. The condition for cooperation agreements (without enforcement) to come about is: $\beta - \gamma 1 - \pi > \beta$, and hence $\pi > \gamma\beta$. On this see also Sugden (2004).

References

Akerlof, G. (1970) "The market for 'lemons': quality uncertainty and the market mechanism," *The Quarterly Journal of Economics*, 84 (3), pp. 488–500.

Anderson, E. (1993) *Value in ethics and in economics*, Harvard University Press, Cambridge, Mass.

Antoci, A., Sacco, P. and Zarri, L. (2004) "Coexistence of strategies and culturally-specific common knowledge: An evolutionary analysis," *Journal of Bioeconomics*, 6, pp. 165–194.

Arendt, H. (1997) *Vita Activa. La Condizione Umana*, Bompiani, Milano.

Aristotle (1996) *Politics*, Oxford University Press, Oxford.

Aristotle (2009) *Nicomachean Ethics*, Oxford University Press, Oxford.

Astley, W. G. and Van de Ven, H. (1983) "Central perspectives and debates in organization theory," *Administrative Science Quarterly*, 28, pp. 245–273.

Axerlod, R. (1984) *The Evolution of Cooperation*, Basic Books.

Ball, P. (2004) *Critical Mass. How one thing leads to another*, Farrar, Straus & Giroux, New York.

Barabasi, A. (2005) *Link*, Einaudi, Torino.

Barrett, R. (2006) *Building a Values-Driven Organization: A Whole System Approach to Cultural Transformation*, Butterworth Heinemann.

Beccaria, C. (1995[1764]) *Dei delitti e delle pene*, Einaudi, Torino.

Bellamy, R. (1987) *Modern Italian Social Theory*, Polity Press, Cambridge.

Bernheim, D. and Stark, O. (1998) "Altruism within the family reconsidered: Do nice guys finish last?," *American Economic Review*, 78 (5), pp. 1034–1045.

Binmore, K. (2005) *Natural Justice*, Oxford University Press, New York.

Binmore, K. (2006) "Why do people cooperate?," *Politics, Philosophy and Economics*, 5 (1), pp. 81–96.

Blume, L. and Durlauf, S. (2000) "The Interaction-Based Approach to Socioeconomic Behavior," *SSRI WP n. 2001*, University of Wisconsin at Madison.

Bomze, I. (1983) "Lotka-Volterra Equation and Replicator Dynamics: A Two-Dimensional Classification," *Biological Cybernetics*, 48, pp. 201–211.

Borzaga, C. and Depedri, S. (2005) "Interpersonal relations and job satisfaction: some empirical results in social and community care services" in Gui and Sugden (2005).

Borzaga, C. and Tortia, E. (2004) "Worker involvement in entrepreneurial nonprofit organizations. Toward a new assessment of workers' perceived satisfaction and fairness" Working Paper n.20, Istituto Studi Sviluppo Aziende Nonprofit, Trento.

Bowles, S. and Gintis, H. (2004) "The evolution of strong reciprocity: cooperation in a heterogeneous population," *Theoretical Population Biology*, 65, pp. 17–28.

Brennan, Geoffrey (1996) "Selection and the currency of reward," in Robert Goodin (ed.) *The Theory of Institutional Design*. Cambridge University Press, Cambridge, pp. 256–275.

Brock, W. and Durlauf, S. (2001) "Discrete Choice with Social Interactions," *Review of Economic Studies*, 68, pp. 235–260.

Brock, W. and Durlauf, S. (2000) "Discrete Choice with Social Interactions," *SSRI WP n. 2007*, University of Wisconsin at Madison.

Bruni, L. (2008) *Reciprocity altruism and civil society*, Routledge, London.

Bruni, L. (2006) *Civil Happiness*, Routledge, London.

Bruni, L. (2012a) *The ethos and genesis of the market*, Macmillan Palvrage, London.

Bruni, L. (2012b) *The wound and the blessing*, Newcity, New York.

Bruni, L. (2013) "On virtues and awards: Giacinto Dragonetti and the tradition of economia civile in enlightenment," *Journal of the History of Economic Thought*, 35 (4), pp. 517–535.

Bruni, L. and Sena, B. (2012) eds, *The Charismatic Principle in Social Life*, Routledge, London.

Bruni, L. and Smerilli, A. (2004) "*I dilemmi dell'individualismo e il paradosso della reciprocità. Ipotesi e giochi*," in Bruni and Crivelli (2004) eds, *Economia e comunione*, Città Nuova, Roma.

Bruni, L. and Smerilli, A. (2008) *Benedetta Economia*, Città Nuova, Roma.

Bruni, L. and A. Smerilli, A. (2009) "The value of vocation. The crucial role of intrinsically motivated people in values-based organizations," in *Review of Social Economy*, 67, pp. 271–288.

Bruni, L. and Smerilli, A. (2010) "Cooperation and diversity," *Munich Working Paper Series*, n. 20564.

Bruni, L. and Smerilli, A. (2012) "Cooperation and diversity: an evolutionary approach," in *Homo Oeconomicus* 29–2, pp. 141–161.

Bruni, L. and Sugden, R. (2000) "Moral canals: trust and social capital in the work of Hume, Smith and Genovesi," *Economics and Philosophy*, 16, pp. 21–45.

Bruni, L. and Sugden, R. (2007) "The road not taken: how psychology was removed from economics, and how it might be brought back," *The Economic Journal*, 117 (516), pp. 146–173.

Bruni, L. and Sugden, R. (2008) "Fraternity. Why the market need not be a morally free zone," in *Economics and Philosophy*, 24, pp. 35–64.

Bruni, L. and Sugden, R. (2013) "Reclaiming Virtue Ethics for Economics," *Journal of Economic Perspectives*, 27 (4), pp. 1–24.

Bruni, L. and Zamagni, S. (2007) *Civil Economy*, Peter Lang, Oxford.

Bruni, L. and Zamagni, S. (2012) (eds) *Handbook on Philanthropy, Social Enterprise and Reciprocity*, E. Elgar, Cheltenham.

Campbell, D. (1995) *Incentives*, Cambridge University Press, Cambridge.

Cialdini, R. (1996) "Social influence and the triple tumor structure of organizational dishonesty." In Messick D. and Tenbrunsel A. (eds) *Codes of conduct: behavioural research into business ethics*, Russell Sage, New York.

Cross, R. and Parker, A. (2004) *The hidden power of social networks*, Harvard Business School Press, Harvard.

Davies, L. (1989) "The institution as an ideological System: How morals make the organization," *Systemic Practice and Action Research*, 2, pp. 287–306.

Davis, J. (ed.) (2001) *The Intersubjectivity in Economics*, Routledge, London.

Deci, E. L. and Ryan, R. M. (1985) *Intrinsic Motivation and Self-Determination in Human Behavior*, Plenum Publishing, New York.

Deci, E. L. and Ryan, R. M. (2002) *Handbook of Self-Determination Research*, University of Rochester Press, Rochester, NY.

Deci, E. (2005) "The Relation of Intrinsic and Extrinsic Goals to Well-being," paper presented at the conference "Capability and Happiness," Milano Bicocca, 17 June 2005.

Delfgaauw, J. and Dur, R. (2004) "Incentives and workers' motivation in the public sector" *Tinbergen Institute Discussion Paper* 04-060/1.

Doria, P. M. (1710) *Della vita civile*, Napoli.

Dragonetti, G. (1769)[1766]) *A treatise on virtues and rewards*, Johnson and Payne, London. First Italian edition [*Delle virtù e de' Premi*], Naples.

Dragonetti, G. (1787[1766]) *Delle virtù e dei premi*, Palermo: Reale Stamperia.

Dragonetti, A. (1847) Le vite degli aquilani illustri, Perchiazzi, L'Aquila.

Dumont, L. (1980) Homo Hierarchicus. The Caste System and Its Implications, Chicago University Press, Chicago (IL).

Durlauf, S. (2001) "A Framework for the Study of Individual Behavior and Social Interaction" *SSRI WP n. 2016R*, University of Wisconsin at Madison.

Esposito, Roberto (2009) *Communitas: the origin and destiny of community*, Stanford: Stanford University Press.

Farrel, D. and Rusbult, C. E. (1992) "Exploring the Exit, Voice, Loyalty, and Neglect Typology: The influence of job satisfaction, quality of alternatives, and investment size," *Employee Responsibilities and Rights Journal*, 5, pp. 201–218.

Fehr, E. and Gächter, S. (2000) "Fairness and Retaliation: The Economics of Reciprocity," *Journal of Economic Perspectives*, 14, p. 159

Fehr, E. and Gächter, S. (2000) "Do Incentive Contracts Crowd Out Voluntary Cooperation?" Working Paper No. 34. *Institute for Empirical Research in Economics Working Paper Series*. Zurich University.

Filangieri, G. (2003)[1780], *La scienza della legislazione*, Grimaldi & C. Editori, Napoli.

Florenskij, P. A. (2006) *Non dimenticatemi. Le lettere dal gulag del grande matematico, filosofo e sacerdote russo*, Mondadori, Milano.

Folbre, N. and Weisskopf, E. (1998) "Did Father Know best? Families, markets, and the supply of caring labour," in *Economics, Values, and Organization*, Cambridge University Press, Cambridge/New York/Melbourne, pp. 171–205.

Folbre, Nancy and Nelson, Julie A. (2000) "For love or money – or both?," *Journal of Economic Perspectives* 14, pp. 123–140.

Frey, Bruno (1997) *Not Just for the Money: An Economic Theory of Personal Motivation*, Edward Elgar.

Frey, B. S. and Gotte, L. (1999) "Does Pay Motivate volunteers?" Unpublished manuscript. *Institute for Empirical Economic Research*. University of Zurich.

Frey, B. and Neckermann, S. (2008) "Awards as Incentives," *IEW – Working Papers 334*, Institute for Empirical Research in Economics – University of Zurich.

Frey, B., Inauen, E., Rost, K. and Osterloh, M. (2009) "Back to the Future – A Monastic Perspective on Corporate Governance" (July 16, 2009). Available at SSRN: http://ssrn.com/abstract=1434814

Genovesi, A. (1962[1767]) *Autobiografia e lettere*, Feltrinelli, Milano.

Genovesi, A. (1973[1766]) *Della diceosina o sia della filosofia del giusto e dell'onesto*, Marzorati, Milano.

Genovesi, A. (1977[1765]) *Scritti*, edited by F. Venturi, Einaudi, Torino.

Genovesi, A. (2005[1765–1767]) *Lezioni di commercio o sia di Economia Civile*, critical edition by M.L. Perna, Istituto Italiano per gli studi filosofici, Napoli.

Gintis, H (2004) "Modeling Cooperation Among Self-Interested Agents: A Critique," *The Journal of Socio-Economics*, 33, pp. 311–322.

Gladwell, M. (2002) *The Tipping Point*, Little, Brown and Company, New York.

Gneezy, U. (2003) "The W effect of incentives," Manuscript.

Gneezy, U. and Rustichini A. (2000a) "A Fine is a Price," *Journal of Legal Studies*, vol. XXIX, 1, part 1, pp. 1–18.

Gneezy, U. and Rustichini, A. (2000b) "Pay Enough or Don't Pay At All." *Quarterly Journal of Economics* August, pp. 791–810.

Granovetter, M. (1978) "Threshold Models of Collective Behavior," *American Journal of Sociology*, 83, pp. 1420–1443.

Granovetter, M. and Soong, R. (1983) "Threshold Models of Diffusion and Collective."

Gui, B. (2002) "Più che scambi, incontri. La teoria economica alle prese con i fenomeni interpersonali," in: Zamagni, Stefano (ed.), *Complessità relazionale e comportamento economico: materiali per un nuovo paradigma di relazionalità*, Bologna, Il Mulino, pp. 15–66.

Gui, B. and R. Sugden (eds) (2005) *Economics and Social Interactions*, Cambridge University Press, Cambridge.

Guzzo, R. and Katzell R. (1987) "Effects od economic incentives on productivity: a psychological view," in Haig R. (ed.), *Incentives, cooperation and risk sharing*, Totowa: Roman and Littlefield, pp. 107–119.

Hargreaves, F. I. and Heap, S. (2000) "Force of conservatism? How to incentivise the public sector," *New economy*, pp. 114–119.

Heckathorn, D. (1996) "The dynamics and dilemmas of collective action," *American Sociological Review*, 61, pp. 250–277.

Heyes, Anthony (2005) "The economics of vocation, or 'Why is a badly-paid nurse a good nurse?'" *Journal of Health Economics*, 24, pp. 561–569.

Heller, W. B. and Sieberg, K. K. (2010) "Honor among thieves: Cooperations as a strategic response to functional unpleasantness," *European Journal of Political Economy*, 26, pp. 351–382.

Hirshleifer, J. and Martinez Coll, J. (1991) "The limits of reciprocity," *Rationality and Society*, 3, pp. 35–64.

Hirschman, A. (1982[1970]) *Exit, Voice and Loyalty. Response to Decline in Firms, Organizations and States*, Harvard University Press, Cambridge (MA).

Hollis, M. (1998) *Trust within reason*, Cambridge University Press.

Jankélévitch, Vladimir (1970) *Traité des vertus*, 3 vols.; vol. II, "Les vertus et l'amour," Bordas, Paris-Montreal.

Katz, Eliakim and Femida Handy (1998) The wage differential between non-profit institutions and corporations: Getting more by paying less? *Journal of Comparative Economics*, 26, pp. 246–261.

Keley, M. (1978) "A Social-Justice Approach to Organizational Evaluation," *Administrative Science Quarterly*, 23, 272–292.

Kolm, S. (2008) *Reciprocity: An economics of social relations*, Cambridge University Press, Cambridge/New York.

Irlenbusch, B. and Sliwka, D. (2003) "Transparency and Reciprocal Behavior in Employment Relations," *IZA Discussion Papers* 887, Institute for the Study of Labor (IZA).

Lane, R. (1991) *The market experience*, Cambridge University Press, Cambridge.

Le Grand, J. (2003) *Motivation, Agency, and Public Policy. Of Knights & Knaves, Pawns & Queens*, Oxford University Press.

Lepper, M. and Greene, R.(1978) *Hidden Costs of Reward: New Perspectives on the Psychology of Human Motivation*, Lawrence Erlbaum Associates, Hillsdale (NJ).

Levi, P. (1997) "L'uomo salvato dal suo mestiere. Intervista di Philip Roth a Primo Levi," in Belpoliti M. (ed.), *Primo Levi: conversazioni e interviste, 1963–1987*, Einaudi, Torino.

Livernois, J and McKenna, C. J. (1999) "Truth or consequences: Enforcing pollution standards with self-reporting," *Journal of Public Economics*, 71, pp. 415–440.

MacIntyre, A. (1981) *After Virtue*. Notre Dame, IN : Notre Dame University Press.

March, J. (1995) *A primer on decision making*, Free Press, New York.

Messick, D. (1999) "Alternative logics for decision making in social settings," *Journal of Economic Behavior and Organization*, 38, pp. 11–28.

Messick, D. and Tenbrunsel, A. (eds) (1999) *Codes of Conduct: Behavioural Research into Business Ethics*, Russell Sage, New York.

Mill, J. S. (1975[1869]) *The Subjection of Women*, Oxford University Press, Oxford.

Minkler, L. (2002) *Shirking and Motivation in Firms: Survey Evidence on Worker Attitudes*, University of Connecticut.

Mitroff, I. I. and Denton, E. A. (1999) "A study of spirituality in the workplace," *Sloan Management Review*, 40 (4), pp. 83–92.

Molteni, M. (2009) "Aziende a movente ideale," in Bruni and Zamagni (eds) pp. 65–75.

Neckermann, S., Cueni, R. and Frey, B. (2009) "What is an Award Worth? An Econometric Assessment of the Impact of Awards on Employee Performance," *CESifo Working Paper Series 2657*, CESifo Group Munich.

Nelson, Julie A. (2005) "Interpersonal relations and economics: comments from a feminist perspective," pp. 250–261 in Benedetto Gui and Robert Sugden (eds) *Economics and Social Interaction: Accounting for Interpersonal Relations*, Cambridge University Press.

Nelson, J. (2009) "A Response to Bruni and Sugden," in *Economics and Philosophy*, 25, pp. 187–193.

Nussbaum, M. (1986) *The Fragility of Goodness: Luck and Ethics in Greek Tragedy and Philosophy*, Cambridge University Press, New York.

Pelligra, V. (2004) "Motivazioni, Procedure e Filtri: strumenti innovative di sviluppo organizzativo" *Dipartimento di Economia, Universita' di Cagliari, mimeo.*

Phelps, A., Adams, R. and Bessant, J. (2007) "Life cycles of growing organizations: A review with implications for knowledge and learning," *International Journal of Management Reviews*, 9, pp. 1–30.

Rawls, J. (1971) *A theory of justice* , Harvard University Press, Harvard.

Ryan, R. (2005) *Basic psychological needs: Arguments and empirical evidence concerning the universal foundations of well being from the perspective of self-determination theory, mimeo*, paper presented at the conference "Capability and Happiness," Milano-Bicocca, 17 June 2005.

Saari, D. G. (2002) "Mathematical social sciences; An Oxymoron?," PIMS distinguished chair lecture, Pacific Institute for Mathematical Sciences.

Sandel, M. (2010) *Justice: What's the Right Thing to Do?* London: Penguin Books.

Sansone, C. and Harackiewicz, J. M. (eds) (2000) *Intrinsic and Extrinsic Motivation: The Search for Optimal Motivation and Performance.* Academic Press, San Diego (CA).

Schelling, T. (1978) *Micromotives and Macrobehavior*, Norton, W. W. & Company, Inc.

Shapiro, A. (2003) *Creating Contagious Commitment*, Strategy Perspective, Hillsborough (NC).

Smerilli, A. (2007) *"We-rationality.* Per una teoria non individualistica della cooperazione," *Economia Politica* 24 (3), pp. 407–425.

Smerilli, A. (2008) "We-thinking and 'double-crossing': frames, reasoning and equilibria," *MPRA Paper 11545*, University Library of Munich, Germany.

Smith A. (1976 [1776]) *The Wealth of Nations*, edited by R.H. Campbell and A.S. Skinner, Oxford University Press, Oxford.

Stanca, L., Bruni, L. and Corazzini, L. (2009) "Testing Theory of Reciprocity," in *Journal of Economic Behavior and Organization*, 71 (2), 233–245.

Sugden, R. (2000) "Team Preferences," *Economics and Philosophy*, 16, pp. 175–204.

Sugden, R. (2003) "The Logic of Team Reasoning," *Philosophical Explorations*, 16, pp. 165–181.

Sugden, R. (2004) The economics of rights, cooperation and welfare, second edition, Palgrave Macmillian, London.

Sugden, R. (2005) "Fellow-Felling," in B. Gui and R. Sugden (eds) *Economics and Social Interactions*, Cambridge University Press, Cambridge.

Teilhard de Chardin, P. (1990) *Sull'amore*, Queriniana, Brescia.

Titmuss, R. M., (1970) *The Gift Relationship*, Allen and Unwin, London.

Uhlaner, C. J. (1989) "Relational goods and participation: incorporating sociality into a theory of rational action," *Public Choice*, 62, pp. 253–285.

Vega-Redondo, F. (1996) Evolution, Games and Economic Behaviour, Oxford University Press, Oxford.

Vega-Redondo, F. (2003) Economics and the Theory of Games, Cambridge University Press, Cambridge.

Walzer, M. (1983) *Spheres of justice. A defence of pluralism and equality*, Basic Books.

Weisbrod (2002) "Volunteer Labor Sorting across Industries," *Journal of Policy Analysis and Management*, 21 (3), pp. 427–447.

Weisbrod, B. (1998) "Modeling the nonprofit organization as a multiproduct firm: A framework for choice," in Weisbrod B. (ed.), *To Profit or Not to Profit. The Commercial Transformation of the Nonprofit Sector*, Cambridge University Press, Cambridge.

Weiss, A. (1980) "Job Queues and Layoffs in Labor Market with Flexible Wages," *The Journal of Political Economy*, 88 (3), pp. 526–538.

Wicksteed, P. H. (1933[1910]) *The Common Sense of Political Economy*, Macmillan, London.

Williamson, O. (1995) *Organization Theory*, Oxford University Press, Oxford.

Withey, M. and Cooper, W. (1989) "Predicting Exit, Voice, Loyalty and Neglect," *Administrative Science Quarterly*, 34, pp. 521–539.

Index

For Product Safety Concerns and Information please contact our EU
representative GPSR@taylorandfrancis.com
Taylor & Francis Verlag GmbH, Kaufingerstraße 24, 80331 München, Germany

www.ingramcontent.com/pod-product-compliance
Ingram Content Group UK Ltd.
Pitfield, Milton Keynes, MK11 3LW, UK
UKHW020934180425
457613UK00019B/392